Kitchen Aid Stand Mixer Cookbook for Beginners

Kitchen Aid Stand Mixer Cookbook for Beginners

Perfect Homemade Recipes and Techniques from My Stand Mixer | Bread, Pasta, Cake, Pie & Tart, Ice Cream, Cookies, and More

Leonard McGrane

The information provided in this book is intended for general informational purposes only and is not a substitute for professional advice. The author and publisher are not responsible for any errors or omissions, or for any action or inaction taken because of the information provided in this book.

The reader assumes full responsibility for all use of this book, including all risks associated with the exercises, programs, and techniques described herein. The author and publisher disclaim all liability for any injury or damage resulting from the use of this book or the exercises, programs, and techniques described herein.

Contents

INTRODUCTION

The KitchenAid stand mixer has stood the test of time as a trusted tool for millions of cooks and bakers worldwide. With its timeless design, powerful performance, and unmatched versatility, this stand mixer isn't just an appliance; it's your partner in creating delicious memories and mastering the art of cooking.

At first glance, the KitchenAid stand mixer may seem like a simple machine, but beneath its sleek exterior lies an engineering marvel capable of tackling countless tasks. It effortlessly mixes, kneads, whips, and blends, taking the heavy lifting out of your kitchen prep. But its true genius lies in its adaptability. With a range of attachments, the stand mixer evolves into a pasta maker, ice cream churner, meat grinder, spiralizer, and more.

The KitchenAid stand mixer is a trusted companion for beginners taking their first steps in baking and for seasoned cooks pushing the boundaries of their creativity.

In this book, we celebrate everything the KitchenAid stand mixer has to offer. Through carefully curated recipes and techniques, you'll discover how this appliance simplifies even the most complex tasks, giving you more time to enjoy the process of creating and sharing incredible food. By the time you finish, you'll not only have mastered the use of your stand mixer but also gained confidence to experiment with new recipes and techniques.

History

The story of the KitchenAid stand mixer begins with an inspired moment of observation and ingenuity in the early 20th century. In 1919, Herbert Johnston, an engineer working for the Hobart Manufacturing Company, noticed a baker laboring to mix dough by hand—a process that was not only time-consuming but also physically demanding. Johnston believed there had to be a better way to streamline this essential kitchen task, and that vision would eventually lead to the creation of one of the most iconic appliances in history.

The First Stand Mixer

Johnston's solution was the Model H, a commercial-grade mixer with a planetary action—the revolutionary design where the attachment spins while rotating around the mixing bowl. This innovation allowed the mixer to handle dough and batter with remarkable efficiency, a feature that remains the hallmark of the KitchenAid stand mixer today.

The Model H was a hit in professional kitchens, but Johnston saw potential for a smaller version suitable for home cooks. After years of research and development, the first household stand mixer, the Model K, was introduced in 1919. It was sleek, efficient, and built to last—a testament to Johnston's engineering expertise.

Why "KitchenAid"?

The name "KitchenAid" came about serendipitously. During product testing, one of the company's executives had his wife try the prototype. After using it, she reportedly exclaimed, "I don't care what you call it—this is the best kitchen aid I've ever had!" The name stuck, perfectly capturing the essence of the appliance.

Innovation

Over the decades, the KitchenAid stand mixer continued to evolve, both in functionality and design. In 1937, industrial designer Egmont Arens reimagined the mixer's appearance, giving it the sleek, curvaceous silhouette we recognize today. This design remains largely unchanged, a testament to its timeless appeal.

As the stand mixer gained popularity, KitchenAid introduced a variety of attachments that transformed it into a multi-functional kitchen powerhouse. From pasta rollers to meat grinders and ice cream makers, the mixer's versatility expanded, making it an essential tool for a wide range of culinary tasks.

A Timeless Icon

Now over a century old, the KitchenAid stand mixer is celebrated worldwide for its quality, durability, and style. Its enduring design and ability to simplify complex kitchen tasks have made it a staple in homes and restaurants alike. For many, owning a KitchenAid stand mixer is a rite of passage, symbolizing a commitment to exploring the joys of cooking and baking.

How to Properly Use

1. Setting Up Your Stand Mixer

Choose the Right Location: Place the stand mixer on a stable, level surface to prevent it from wobbling during use.

Attach the Bowl: Secure the mixing bowl to the base. Tilt-head models require you to twist the bowl into place, while bowl-lift models use a lever to raise the bowl into position.

2. Preparing Ingredients

Measure Accurately: Use proper measuring tools for dry and wet ingredients to ensure recipe success.

Room Temperature Ingredients: For most recipes, such as cakes or cookies, ingredients like butter and eggs should be at room temperature to mix evenly.

3. Using the Speed Settings

The KitchenAid stand mixer has multiple speed settings. Here's a general guide:

Speed 1 (Stir): Gentle mixing to prevent splattering. Great for incorporating flour or other dry ingredients.

Speed 2 (Slow Mix): For heavier mixtures like bread dough or mashed potatoes.

Speed 4–6 (Medium Mix): Ideal for creaming butter and sugar, mixing cake batters, or whipping mashed potatoes.

Speed 8–10 (Fast Mix/Whip): For whipping cream or beating egg whites to stiff peaks.

4. Step-by-Step Mixing

Start Slowly: Begin on the lowest speed to prevent ingredients from flying out of the bowl. Gradually increase the speed as the ingredients combine.

Scrape the Bowl: Use a spatula to scrape down the sides of the bowl periodically to ensure all ingredients are evenly mixed.

Monitor Consistency: Avoid overmixing, especially for delicate recipes like cakes or whipped cream, as this can affect the texture.

5. Using Attachments

The KitchenAid stand mixer comes with optional attachments that expand its capabilities:

Flat Beater: Used for most baking recipes like cakes, cookies, and quick breads (e.g., Honey Oatmeal Bread, Chocolate Chunk Brownies, Cheesecake). It's ideal for mixing batters and doughs that don't need heavy kneading or whipping.

Wire Whisk: Perfect for incorporating air into ingredients, ideal for whipped cream, meringues, or light batters like Chocolate Babka and Panna Cotta. It can also be used for egg whites and other fluffy mixtures.

Dough Hook: Essential for bread and pizza doughs, such as Honey Oatmeal Bread, Pasta Carbonara dough, and Fettuccine. It mimics hand-kneading, making it easier to develop gluten in the dough.

Pasta Roller and Cutter Set: Includes attachments like the Pasta Roller and Fettuccine Cutter. These attachments are necessary for rolling and cutting pasta dough, used in recipes like Ricotta Tortellini, Tagliatelle, and Gnocchi.

Food Grinder: Used for grinding meat or vegetables. In the case of recipes like Sausage and Swedish Meatballs, this attachment is helpful for grinding fresh meat and other ingredients to create your own fillings.

Ice Cream Maker Attachment: Used for making frozen treats like Mango Sorbet and Frozen Yogurt. It allows you to churn and freeze mixtures directly in the stand mixer, offering an efficient way to create homemade ice cream and sorbet.

Spiralizer: Create vegetable noodles or slices.

Before using any attachment with your KitchenAid stand mixer, ensure the mixer is off and unplugged. Insert the attachment into the power hub, aligning the prongs with the hub. Secure it by turning or locking it in place. Gently pull the attachment to confirm it's properly attached. Once locked in, plug in the mixer, set the speed, and you're ready to go.

6. Cleaning and Maintenance

Unplug First: Always unplug the mixer before cleaning or switching attachments.

Hand Wash Parts: The bowl, beaters, and other removable parts can be hand-washed with warm, soapy water.

Wipe the Body: Clean the mixer's body with a damp cloth to remove spills. Avoid immersing the motor base in water.

Keep the Hub Area Clean: The hub (where the attachments are inserted) should be kept free from food debris. Wipe it with a damp cloth after each use. Be careful not to get any water into the attachment area, as this could cause electrical or mechanical issues.

Inspect Regularly: Check for loose parts or wear and tear to ensure it remains in optimal condition.

7. Safety Tips

Do Not Overfill: Overloading the bowl can strain the motor and result in uneven mixing.

Lock the Head/Bowl: Ensure the tilt-head is locked in place or the bowl is secured in bowl-lift models before use.

Keep Hands Away from Moving Parts: Never insert hands or utensils into the bowl while the mixer is running. Always turn off the mixer before scraping the sides or making adjustments.

Supervise Usage: Never leave the mixer running unattended, especially at high speeds.

Benefits of this Stand Mixer

The KitchenAid stand mixer is more than just a mixing tool—it's a multifunctional kitchen companion. Here's a list of what can be achieved with it:

- Whipping to Perfection

Create light and airy mixtures effortlessly with the whisk attachment. Whip cream, mashed potatoes, or eggs to the perfect consistency, ideal for mousses, soufflés, and meringues. Desserts like tiramisu or homemade whipped cream for toppings are a breeze with the mixer's high-speed settings.

- Process Food

Slice, shred, or julienne fruits and vegetables with the food processor attachment, saving time in meal prep. You can even peel, core, and spiralize fresh produce, making this attachment perfect for creating everything from salads to salsas.

- Grind and Stuff with Precision

Transform your stand mixer into a grinder for meats, cheeses, and breadcrumbs using the metal grinder attachment. Create fresh burger patties, falafels, or even stuffed sausages with the sausage stuffer kit, tailoring flavors to suit your taste.

- Homemade Pasta Made Simple

Roll out fresh pasta dough with the pasta roller attachment and cut it into perfect fettuccine, spaghetti, or ravioli. For a fun twist, experiment with colorful pasta varieties, such as beet-infused noodles.

- Knead Dough

Skip the effort of hand-kneading with the dough hook, perfect for bread, pizza crusts, and pastries. Achieve evenly mixed dough without the physical strain, allowing you to focus on perfecting your recipes.

- Shredding Made Quick

Shred warm, cooked chicken or pork in minutes using the flat beater attachment. This is ideal for tacos, pulled pork sandwiches, or barbecue recipes, saving you valuable time in the kitchen.

- Make Homemade Juice

The juicer attachment enables you to extract fresh, homemade juices from fruits and vegetables. With customizable pulp settings, you can create everything from refreshing morning orange juice to creative cocktail mixers.

- Mix Batters

Stand mixers ensure smooth and consistent batters for cakes, pancakes, and waffles. Use them to explore exciting recipes like chai-spiced carrot cake, crepes, or molten lava cakes, achieving flawless textures every time.

- Homemade Ice Cream

With the ice cream maker attachment, indulge in custom creations like Thai tea or lavender honey ice cream. Add fruits, cookies, or chocolates to craft your unique frozen desserts.

- Shave Ice Treats

Cool off on summer days with the shave ice attachment. Create fluffy, snow-like textures for desserts and beverages, from citrusy lemon lavender treats to unique coffee-based creations.

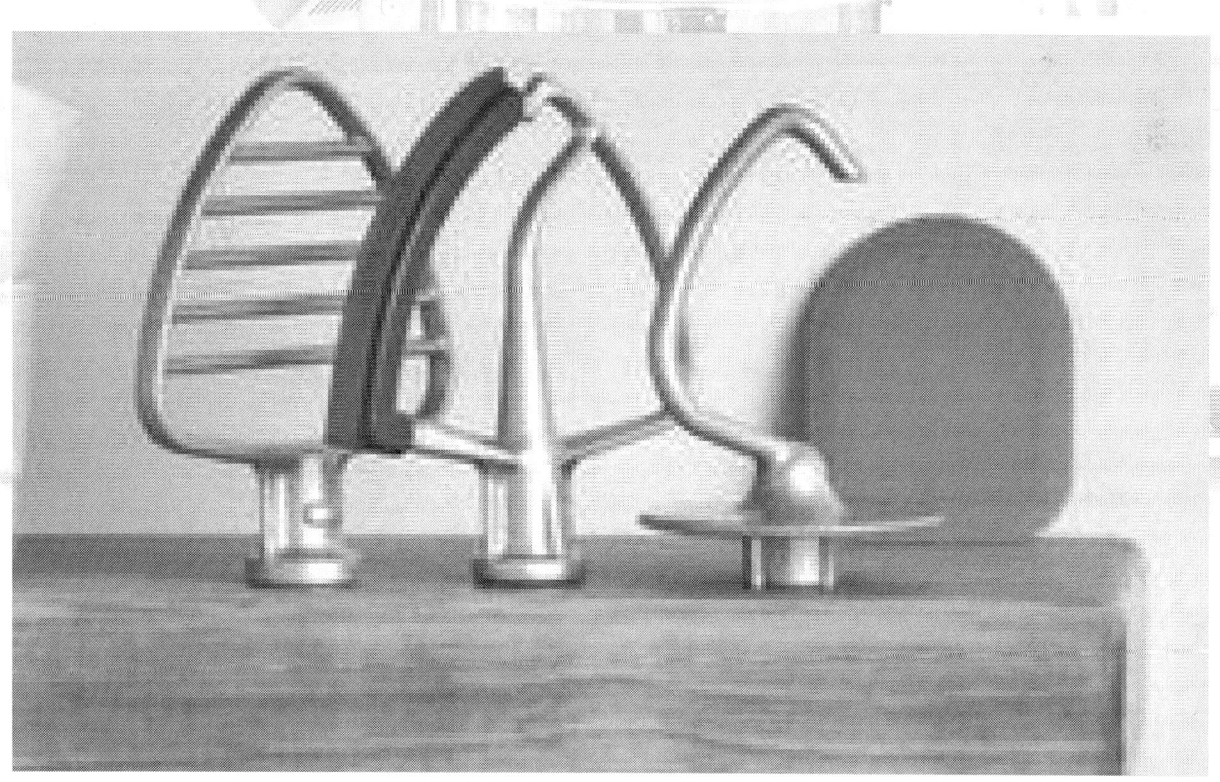

BREAD

1. Rye Bread
2. Sandwich Bread
3. Banana Bread
4. Bavarian Pretzels
5. Rosemary Garlic Pull Apart Bread
6. Pork and Apple Bedfordshire Clangers
7. Seeded Challah
8. Whole Wheat Bread
9. Sourdough Bread
10. Multigrain Loaf
11. Chocolate Babka
12. Brioche
13. Focaccia with Toppings
14. Honey Oatmeal Bread

Rye Bread

Ingredients:

1 ½ cups warm water (110°F/45°C) | 2 tsp active dry yeast | 1 tbsp honey or sugar | 1 ½ cups rye flour | 2 ½ cups all-purpose flour | 1 ½ tsp salt | 1 tbsp olive oil (or vegetable oil) | 1 tbsp caraway seeds (optional, for traditional flavor) | 1 tbsp vital wheat gluten (optional, for a lighter texture)

Total Time: Approximately 2 hours

Servings: 1 medium loaf (8–10 slices)

Directions:

1. In a small bowl, combine warm water, honey (or sugar), and yeast. Stir gently and let it sit for about 5-10 minutes until the mixture becomes frothy.
2. Combine Dry Ingredients: Attach the **Flat Beater** to your stand mixer. In the mixer's bowl, combine rye flour, all-purpose flour, salt, and optional vital wheat gluten. Stir to combine.
3. Add the activated yeast mixture, olive oil, and caraway seeds (if using) to the dry ingredients in the stand mixer bowl. Begin mixing on low speed (setting 2) for about 2 minutes to incorporate the ingredients. You'll notice the dough starting to come together.
4. Switch to the **Dough Hook attachment** and knead the dough on medium speed (setting 4) for about 8–10 minutes. If the dough feels too sticky, add a tablespoon of flour at a time. If it's too dry, add a teaspoon of water at a time. Aim for a soft, elastic dough that doesn't stick excessively to the sides of the bowl.
5. Remove the dough from the bowl and lightly oil it. Form it into a ball and place it back into the bowl. Cover with a clean kitchen towel and let it rise in a warm place for about 1 to 1 ½ hours, or until the dough doubles in size.
6. After the dough has risen, punch it down to release the air. Remove the dough from the bowl and shape it into a loaf by folding the edges inward and rolling it into a tight cylinder.

7. Place the shaped dough into a greased loaf pan, covering it with a towel. Let it rise again for about 30-45 minutes, or until the dough rises slightly above the top of the loaf pan. While the dough is rising, preheat your oven to 375°F (190°C).
8. Once the dough has risen, bake it in the preheated oven for 35-40 minutes, or until the top is golden brown and the loaf sounds hollow when tapped on the bottom. If you have a thermometer, the internal temperature should be around 190°F (88°C).

Nutritional Info (per slice):

Calories: 150 | Carbohydrates: 30g | Protein: 4g | Fat: 2g | Fiber: 4g | Sodium: 300mg

Tips:

- ✓ Traditional rye bread often includes caraway seeds for added flavor. If you don't like caraway seeds, you can skip them or substitute with fennel seeds for a different flavor.
- ✓ Rye bread tends to be denser and will stay fresh for about 3-4 days when stored in a bread box or sealed container. For longer storage, slice the bread and freeze it.

Sandwich Bread

Ingredients

3 ¾ cups (450g) bread flour | 2 tablespoons sugar | 2 teaspoons salt | 2 ¼ teaspoons (1 packet) instant yeast | 1 ¼ cups (300ml) warm milk (about 110°F/45°C) | 2 tablespoons unsalted butter, softened | 1 egg (optional, for richer dough)

Total Time: 2 hours 40 minutes to 3 hours

Servings: Makes 1 loaf (about 10-12 slices).

Directions

1. Attach the dough hook to your stand mixer. In the mixer bowl, combine the bread flour, sugar, salt, and instant yeast. Pour the warm milk and softened butter into the bowl. If using an egg, add it now.
2. Turn the stand mixer to speed 2 and mix until the ingredients form a shaggy dough, about 2-3 minutes. Increase to speed 4 and knead for 8-10 minutes until the dough is smooth, elastic, and slightly tacky to the touch. If the dough is too sticky, add a tablespoon of flour at a time until manageable.
3. Remove the dough from the bowl and form it into a ball. Lightly grease the bowl, place the dough back in, and cover with plastic wrap or a damp towel. Let it rise in a warm place until doubled in size, about 1 hour.
4. Gently deflate the dough and transfer it to a floured surface. Roll it into a rectangle, then tightly roll it into a log. Pinch the seam closed.
5. Place the dough seam-side down in a greased loaf pan. Cover and let it rise again until it reaches about 1 inch above the pan, 30-45 minutes.
6. Preheat the oven to 375°F (190°C). Bake for 30-35 minutes or until the top is golden brown and the loaf sounds hollow when tapped.

Nutritional Info (per slice)

Calories: 160 | Protein: 4g | Carbohydrates: 27g | Fat: 4g | Fiber: 1g

Banana Bread

Ingredients

2 to 3 ripe bananas, mashed | ½ cup (115g) unsalted butter, softened | ¾ cup (150g) granulated sugar | 2 large eggs | 1 tsp vanilla extract | 1¾ cups (220g) all-purpose flour | 1 tsp baking soda | ¼ tsp salt | ½ cup (120ml) buttermilk or plain yogurt | Optional: ½ cup chopped walnuts or chocolate chips

Total Time: 75 minutes

Servings: 1 loaf (approximately 8-10 slices)

Directions

1. Preheat your oven to 350°F (175°C). Grease and flour a standard loaf pan.
2. Use the flat beater attachment with the stand mixer on low speed to mash the bananas until the lumps disappear. Set aside.
3. With the paddle attachment, add softened butter and sugar in the mixer bowl. Beat on medium speed for 2-3 minutes, or until the mixture is light and fluffy. Reduce the mixer speed to low. Add the eggs, one at a time. Mix in the vanilla extract.
4. Combine Dry Ingredients: In a separate bowl, whisk together the flour, baking soda, and salt.
5. Gradually add the dry ingredients to the mixer bowl, alternating with the buttermilk. Begin and end with the dry ingredients. Mix on low speed to avoid overmixing, scraping down the sides of the bowl as needed.
6. Fold in the mashed bananas using the mixer on the lowest setting or by hand with a spatula. If using walnuts or chocolate chips, fold them in gently.
7. Pour the batter into the prepared loaf pan and smooth the top. Bake for 55-65 minutes, or until a toothpick inserted into the center comes out clean.

Nutritional Information (per slice)

Calories: ~210 | Protein: 3g | Carbohydrates: 32g | Fat: 8g | Fiber: 1g | Sugar: 15g

Bavarian Pretzels

Ingredients:

4 ½ cups (540g) bread flour | 2 ¼ tsp (1 packet) active dry yeast | 1 ½ tsp salt | 1 tbsp granulated sugar | 1 ½ cups (360ml) warm water (about 110°F or 45°C) | 2 tbsp unsalted butter, melted | ½ cup (120g) baking soda (for boiling) | 8 cups (2 liters) water (for boiling) | Coarse salt for sprinkling

Total Time: ~1 hour 40 minutes

Servings: Makes 8 large pretzels.

Directions:

1. In a small bowl, combine warm water, sugar, and yeast. Let sit for 5 minutes until the mixture is frothy.
2. Attach the dough hook to your stand mixer. In the mixing bowl, combine bread flour and salt. Add the activated yeast mixture and melted butter. Turn the mixer to low speed and mix until the dough begins to come together. Increase to medium speed and knead for 6-8 minutes until the dough is smooth and elastic.
3. Remove the dough from the bowl, shape it into a ball, and lightly grease the mixing bowl with oil. Place the dough back in the bowl and cover with a clean kitchen towel. Let it rise in a warm place for about 1 hour or until doubled in size.
4. Preheat your oven to 425°F (220°C) and line two baking sheets with parchment paper. Divide the dough into 8 equal pieces. Roll each piece into a 20-inch rope, then twist into a pretzel shape.
5. In a large pot, bring 8 cups of water to a boil. Slowly add baking soda, stirring to dissolve. Gently drop each pretzel into the baking soda bath, one or two at a time, for 30 seconds. Remove with a slotted spoon and place on the prepared baking sheets.

6. Sprinkle coarse salt over the pretzels and bake for 12-15 minutes or until deep golden brown.
7. Let pretzels cool slightly before serving. Pair with mustard or cheese sauce for an authentic touch.

Nutritional Information (per pretzel)

Calories: 220 | Total Fat: 3g | Saturated Fat: 1g | Cholesterol: 5mg | Sodium: 520mg (varies depending on salt used) | Total Carbohydrates: 42g | Dietary Fiber: 2g | Sugars: 2g | Protein: 6g

Rosemary Garlic Pull Apart Bread

Ingredients

Bread Dough: 3 ¾ cups (470 g) all-purpose flour | 2 ¼ tsp (7 g) instant yeast (1 packet) | 1 ½ tsp salt | 1 tbsp sugar | 1 ¼ cups (300 ml) warm milk (110°F/45°C) | 1 large egg, room temperature | ¼ cup (60 g) unsalted butter, softened

Garlic-Rosemary Butter: 4 tbsp (60 g) unsalted butter, melted | 2 cloves garlic, minced | 2 tbsp fresh rosemary, finely chopped

Total Time: ~2 hours 20 minutes

Servings: Makes 12 servings

Directions

1. Attach the dough hook to your stand mixer. In the mixer bowl, combine warm milk, sugar, and yeast. Let it sit for 5 minutes until foamy (to activate the yeast), then add the flour, salt, egg, and softened butter to the bowl.

2. Start the mixer on low speed until the ingredients are combined. Increase the speed to medium and knead for 5-7 minutes until the dough becomes smooth and elastic. If the dough is sticky, add flour 1 tbsp at a time.
3. Lightly grease the mixing bowl, place the dough inside, and cover it with a damp towel. Let it rise in a warm place for about 1 hour or until doubled in size.
4. Punch down the risen dough and transfer it to a floured surface. Divide the dough into 12 equal pieces. Shape each piece into a ball.
5. Prepare the garlic-rosemary butter by mixing the melted butter, minced garlic, and chopped rosemary.
6. Dip each dough ball into the garlic-rosemary butter and place it into a greased 9x5-inch loaf pan or a round baking dish, slightly overlapping each piece. Pour any remaining butter over the assembled dough. Cover the pan with a towel and let the dough rise for 30 minutes, until puffy.
7. Preheat your oven to 350°F (175°C). Bake for 25-30 minutes, or until the top is golden brown and the bread sounds hollow when tapped.

Nutritional Information (per serving)

Calories: ~210 | Protein: 5g | Fat: 9g | Carbohydrates: 27g | Fiber: 1g | Sodium: 250mg

Tips: For a crispier crust, brush the bread with a little milk before baking.

Pork and Apple Bedfordshire Clangers

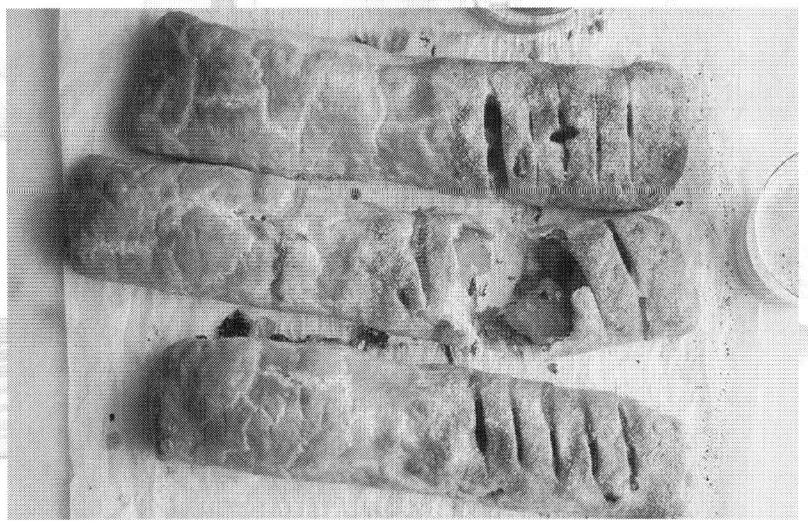

Ingredients

For the Dough: 2 cups (250g) all-purpose flour | 1 tsp salt | ½ tsp baking powder | ½ cup (115g) cold butter, diced | ¼ cup (60ml) water (cold)| 1 egg, beaten (for brushing the clangers)

For the Filling: 1 lb (450g) ground pork | 1 medium apple, peeled, cored, and grated | ½ small onion, finely chopped | ½ tsp ground black pepper | ½ tsp salt | ½ tsp ground sage (optional) | 1 tbsp olive oil (for sautéing the onion)

Total Time: 55 minutes

Servings: Makes 4 large clangers

Directions

1. Attach the flat beater to your stand mixer. Add the flour, salt, and baking powder to the mixer bowl. Add the diced butter to the flour mixture. Turn the mixer on to low speed and mix until the butter is broken down into small pea-sized pieces.
2. Gradually add the cold water while the mixer is running on low speed until the dough just comes together. It should be firm but not too sticky.
3. Turn the dough out onto a lightly floured surface and knead the dough briefly by hand to bring it together into a ball. Wrap the dough in plastic wrap and refrigerate it while you prepare the filling.
4. Prepare the Filling: Heat the olive oil in a pan over medium heat. Add the chopped onion and sauté until softened and translucent (about 3-4 minutes). Add the ground pork, grated apple, salt, pepper, and optional sage. Cook until the pork is browned and fully cooked through, breaking up the meat with a spoon. Allow the mixture to cool slightly before using.
5. Preheat your oven to 375°F (190°C) and line a baking sheet with parchment paper.
6. Roll out the dough on a floured surface to about ¼ inch (0.6 cm) thickness. Cut the dough into rectangles (approximately 5x7 inches or 12x17 cm). Spoon a portion of the pork and apple filling into the center of each rectangle. Fold the dough over the filling to form a pocket, pinching the edges to seal the clanger.
7. Transfer the filled clangers to the prepared baking sheet and brush the tops with the beaten egg to give them a golden finish.
8. Bake the clangers in the preheated oven for 25-30 minutes or until the pastry is golden brown and cooked through.

Tip: These clangers can be frozen before baking. Just wrap them tightly in plastic wrap and place them in an airtight container. When ready to bake, place the frozen clangers directly on a baking sheet and add an extra 10 minutes of baking time.

Nutritional Information (per serving):

Calories: ~350 kcal | Carbohydrates: 30g | Protein: 20g | Fat: 20g | Fiber: 2g | Sodium: 500mg

Seeded Challah

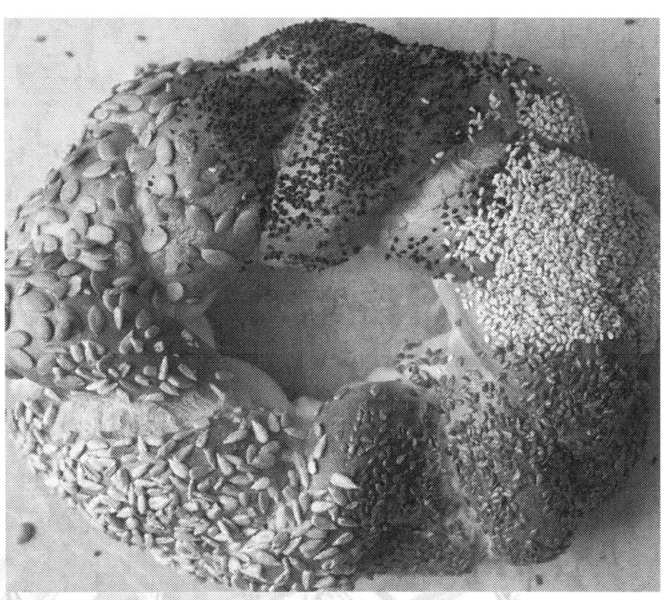

Ingredients:

1 packet (2 ¼ tsp) active dry yeast | ¼ cup warm water | 1 tbsp honey | 2 large eggs | 2 tbsp vegetable oil | 3 ½ cups all-purpose flour, divided | 1 tsp salt | ½ cup warm milk (about 110°F) | ¼ cup sunflower seeds | ¼ cup sesame seeds | ¼ cup poppy seeds | 1 egg, beaten (for egg wash)

Active Time: 15 minutes

Total Time: 2 hours 45 minutes

Servings: Makes 1 large loaf (about 10-12 servings)

Directions:

1. In a small bowl, dissolve the honey in the warm water. Sprinkle the active dry yeast over the top and let it sit for about 5 minutes, until it becomes foamy.
2. Attach the flat beater to the mixer. Pour the yeast mixture into the mixing bowl of your stand mixer.
3. Add the eggs, warm milk, and vegetable oil into the mixing bowl with the yeast mixture. Mix on low speed for about 30 seconds until combined. Gradually add the flour (reserve about ½ cup for kneading) and salt to the mixing bowl.
4. Switch to the dough hook attachment. Mix on low speed for about 3-4 minutes until the dough comes together. Increase the speed to medium-low and knead the dough for about 8-10 minutes. Add the remaining flour gradually if the dough feels too sticky. Once kneaded, the dough should be soft but not sticky, and should spring back when pressed.
5. Place the dough in a greased bowl, turning it to coat it with a thin layer of oil. Cover the bowl with a clean kitchen towel or plastic wrap. Let the dough rise in a warm place for 1-1.5 hours or until it doubles in size.

6. Once the dough has risen, punch it down to release air bubbles. Divide the dough into three even pieces. Roll each piece into a long rope and braid them together into a traditional three-strand challah. Pinch the ends together and tuck them under the loaf.
7. Place the braided dough on a greased baking sheet or lined with parchment paper. Cover the dough with a towel and let it rise for another 30 minutes.
8. Brush the loaf with the beaten egg wash to create a shiny, golden crust. Sprinkle the top with a mixture of sunflower, sesame, and poppy seeds for added flavor and crunch.
9. Preheat the oven to 350°F (175°C). Bake the loaf for 30-35 minutes or until golden brown.

Nutritional Information (per serving, approximate):

Calories: 180 | Protein: 5g | Carbohydrates: 28g | Fat: 5g | Fiber: 2g

Whole Wheat Bread

Ingredients

3 cups whole wheat flour | 1 cup all-purpose flour | 2 tablespoons honey (or maple syrup for a subtle sweetness) | 1 ½ teaspoons salt | 1 tablespoon instant yeast | 1 ¼ cups warm water (about 110°F / 43°C) | 2 tablespoons olive oil (or vegetable oil) | 1 tablespoon molasses (optional for added depth of flavor)

Total Time: 45–45 minutes

Servings: 1 loaf (8–10 slices)

Directions

1. In the bowl of your stand mixer, combine the warm water, honey (or maple syrup), and molasses (if using). Sprinkle the instant yeast over the water and let it sit for about 5–10 minutes, until it becomes frothy.
2. Mix the dry ingredients: In a separate bowl, mix the whole wheat flour, all-purpose flour, and salt.
3. Attach the flat beater attachment to the stand mixer. Add the dry ingredients to the yeast mixture in the mixer bowl. Start mixing on a low speed (Speed 2) for 1-2 minutes until everything is well combined. Add the olive oil to the dough mixture and continue mixing for another 1-2 minutes on medium speed (Speed 4).
4. Switch to the dough hook attachment on your stand mixer. Start kneading the dough at low speed (Speed 2) for about 8-10 minutes. If the dough is too sticky, sprinkle a bit more flour—1 tablespoon at a time.
5. Remove the dough from the bowl and lightly grease the mixing bowl with a little olive oil. Place the dough back in the bowl, cover it with a clean kitchen towel, and let it rise for 1–1.5 hours, or until it doubles in size. You can also place it in a warm spot to speed up the process.
6. Once the dough has risen, punch it down to release the air. Turn it out onto a lightly floured surface and shape it into a loaf. If you prefer a round shape, shape it into a round boule. For a classic loaf, form it into a rectangular shape.
7. Grease your loaf pan (8x4 inches or 9x5 inches). Place the shaped dough into the pan and cover it with a towel. Let it rise for another 30-45 minutes, until the dough has risen just above the lip of the pan.
8. Preheat your oven to 375°F (190°C). Place the loaf in the oven and bake for 30-35 minutes, or until the top is golden brown, and the loaf sounds hollow when tapped on the bottom. The internal temperature should be around 190°F (88°C).

Nutritional Information (per slice)

Calories: 120 | Carbs: 22g | Protein: 4g | Fat: 2g | Fiber: 4g | Sugar: 3g

Sourdough Bread

Ingredients

500g (4 cups) all-purpose flour | 350ml (1 ½ cups) warm water | 100g (½ cup) active sourdough starter | 10g (1 ½ teaspoons) salt | 1 tablespoon olive oil (optional, for softer crust) | 1 teaspoon honey or sugar (optional, to help feed the starter)

Preparation Time: 15 minutes

Baking Time: 45-50 minutes

Total Time: Approximately 10 hours (including proofing)

Servings: 1 large loaf (8-10 servings)

Directions

1. Attach the flat beater to the stand mixer. In the mixer bowl, combine the flour, salt, and honey (if using). Stir together on low speed until evenly mixed. Add the sourdough starter and warm water to the bowl. Stir on low speed using the flat beater until a shaggy dough forms. This usually takes about 2-3 minutes.
2. Switch to the dough hook attachment. Set the mixer to medium-low speed and knead the dough for about 6-8 minutes. If the dough is too sticky, add a small amount of flour, 1 tablespoon at a time. If it's too dry, add a little water until you achieve a tacky but not sticky consistency.
3. Lightly oil the mixing bowl or coat it with non-stick spray. Place the dough in the bowl, cover it with a damp cloth, and let it rise in a warm area for 8-12 hours (or overnight). The dough should roughly double in size.
4. After the first proof, punch the dough down to release excess air. Turn the dough out onto a lightly floured surface. Gently shape it into a round or oval loaf, depending on your preference.

5. Transfer the shaped dough onto a parchment-lined baking sheet or into a proofing basket (banneton). Cover with a damp towel or plastic wrap. Let the dough rise for another 1-2 hours, or until it has nearly doubled in size.
6. Preheat your oven to 475°F (245°C). Once the oven is hot, score the top of the dough with a sharp knife or bread lame to help it expand as it bakes. Bake for 30 minutes with the lid on (or covered with a metal bowl) to create steam. This helps develop a crispy, golden crust.
7. After 30 minutes, remove the lid (if using) and bake for another 15-20 minutes until the loaf is golden brown and sounds hollow when tapped on the bottom.

Nutritional Information (per serving)

Calories: 160 | Carbohydrates: 32g | Protein: 5g | Fat: 1g | Fiber: 1g | Sugar: 1g

Tips: For a more artisan-style crust, place a pan of water on the bottom rack of the oven while baking to create steam.

Multigrain Loaf

Ingredients

1 cup warm water (110°F/43°C) | 1 tablespoon active dry yeast | 2 tablespoons honey | 2 tablespoons olive oil | 1 ½ cups whole wheat flour | 1 cup all-purpose flour | ½ cup rolled oats | ½ cup sunflower seeds | ¼ cup flaxseeds | 1 teaspoon salt | 1 tablespoon vital wheat gluten (optional, for a lighter loaf)

Prep Time: 15 minutes

Cook Time: 35-40 minutes

Servings: 10 slices

Directions

1. In the bowl of the stand mixer, combine the warm water, honey, and active dry yeast. Stir gently using the dough hook attachment until mixed. Let the mixture sit for 5-10 minutes until it becomes frothy.
2. Combine the Dry Ingredients: In a separate bowl, whisk together the whole wheat flour, all-purpose flour, rolled oats, sunflower seeds, flaxseeds, and salt.
3. Once the yeast mixture is ready, add the dry ingredients to the KitchenAid bowl. Attach the dough hook and set the mixer to low speed (Speed 2) to combine. Once the flour is incorporated, increase the speed to medium (Speed 4) for about 7-10 minutes. Let the stand mixer knead the dough until it becomes smooth and elastic.
4. Lightly oil a large bowl. Transfer the dough into the bowl, cover with a clean kitchen towel, and let it rise for 1 hour or until it doubles in size.
5. Once the dough has risen, punch it down to remove air bubbles. Lightly flour a surface and shape the dough into a loaf. Place it into a greased loaf pan, pressing it down gently to fit the pan.
6. Cover the loaf with a towel and let it rise again for 30 minutes to 1 hour, or until it has risen above the edge of the loaf pan.
7. Preheat the oven to 375°F (190°C). Bake the bread for 35-40 minutes, or until the top is golden brown and the loaf sounds hollow when tapped on the bottom. You can also check the internal temperature with a kitchen thermometer; it should read 190°F (88°C).

Nutritional Value (per serving, 1 slice)

Calories: 120 | Carbohydrates: 22g | Protein: 4g | Fat: 3g | Fiber: 4g | Sodium: 200mg | Sugar: 4g

Chocolate Babka

Ingredients

For the Dough: 3 ½ cups all-purpose flour | ½ cup sugar | 1 teaspoon salt | 2 teaspoons active dry yeast | ½ cup warm milk (110°F/45°C) | 2 large eggs | ½ cup unsalted butter, softened | 1 teaspoon vanilla extract | ½ cup lukewarm water (for activating yeast)

For the Filling: 1 cup semi-sweet chocolate chips | ½ cup unsalted butter | 2 tablespoons cocoa powder | ½ cup powdered sugar | 1 teaspoon vanilla extract

For the Egg Wash: 1 egg, beaten | 1 tablespoon water

Prep Time: 30 minutes

Proofing Time: 1 to 1 ½ hours

Baking Time: 30 35 minutes

Servings: Makes 1 large loaf (about 8-10 servings)

Directions

1. In the mixer bowl, combine warm water and sugar. Sprinkle the yeast over the top and let it sit for 5-10 minutes until it becomes foamy.
2. Add the flour, salt, eggs, milk, and vanilla to the activated yeast mixture. Attach the dough hook to the stand mixer. Mix on low speed (Speed 2) until the dough comes together. Increase the speed to medium (Speed 4) and knead for about 8-10 minutes until the dough is smooth and elastic.
3. Gradually add the softened butter, a few tablespoons at a time, and continue mixing until fully incorporated. The dough will become sticky but should start to pull away from the sides of the bowl.

4. Remove the dough from the bowl and shape it into a ball. Lightly oil the bowl, return the dough to it, and cover with a damp cloth or plastic wrap. Let the dough rise in a warm place for 1-1.5 hours, or until doubled in size.
5. Prepare the Filling: In a small saucepan over low heat, melt the butter and chocolate, stirring until smooth. Remove from heat and whisk in the cocoa powder, powdered sugar, and vanilla extract. Let it cool to room temperature.
6. Punch the risen dough down and transfer it to a lightly floured surface. Roll the dough into a rectangle (about 14"x10").
7. Spread the cooled chocolate filling evenly over the dough, leaving a small border around the edges. Roll the dough tightly from the longer side into a log.
8. Cut the dough in half lengthwise to expose the chocolate swirl. Carefully twist the two pieces of dough together, keeping the swirled side facing outward. Form the twisted dough into a loaf shape and place it in a greased 9x5-inch loaf pan.
9. Cover the pan with a cloth and let the dough rise for another 30-45 minutes until it's puffy.
10. Preheat your oven to 350°F (175°C). Brush the top of the babka with the beaten egg and water mixture for a glossy finish. Bake the babka for 30-35 minutes or until golden brown and a toothpick inserted comes out clean. You can cover the loaf with foil if it's browning too quickly.

Nutritional Info (per serving)

Calories: 320 | Fat: 18g | Carbs: 39g | Protein: 5g | Sugar: 15g

Tips: Feel free to add chopped nuts (like walnuts or hazelnuts) to the filling for an extra crunch.

Brioche

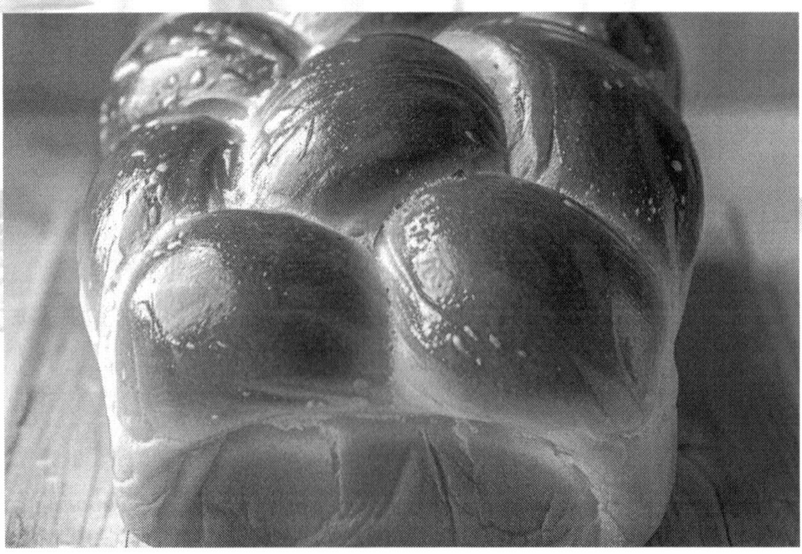

Ingredients

4 cups (480g) all-purpose flour | ¼ cup (50g) granulated sugar | 1 teaspoon salt | 1 tablespoon active dry yeast | 5 large eggs, at room temperature | 1 cup (230g) unsalted butter, softened | ¼ cup (60ml) warm milk | 1 tablespoon honey | 1 egg (for egg wash)

Prep Time: 15 minutes

Cook Time: 25-30 minutes (for baking)

Servings: Makes 1 loaf (12-14 slices)

Directions

1. In the bowl of the stand mixer, combine warm milk (around 110°F) with honey. Stir to dissolve. Sprinkle the active dry yeast over the top of the milk mixture and let it sit for about 5 minutes until frothy.
2. Mix the Dry Ingredients: Using the flat beater attachment, add the all-purpose flour, sugar, and salt into the mixer bowl. Mix on low speed to combine. Once the yeast mixture is activated, gradually add it into the dry ingredients.
3. Add the eggs one at a time, mixing on low speed until fully incorporated. The mixture will be slightly sticky at this point. With the mixer running on low speed, gradually add the softened butter, a few tablespoons at a time. Once all the butter has been added, switch to medium speed.
4. Knead the dough using the stand mixer's dough hook attachment for about 8-10 minutes. The dough will be soft and sticky but should hold together well.
5. Lightly grease a bowl and place the dough in it, turning it once to coat it in oil. Cover with a damp cloth or plastic wrap and let it rise in a warm place for about 1.5-2 hours, or until doubled in size.
6. Once the dough has risen, punch it down to release the air. Turn the dough out onto a floured surface and shape it into a loaf or divide it into smaller portions for individual rolls. Place the shaped dough into a greased loaf pan or arrange the rolls on a baking sheet.
7. Cover the dough again and allow it to rise for another hour or until doubled in size.
8. Preheat the oven to 375°F (190°C). Beat the remaining egg with a tablespoon of water and brush the egg wash over the top of the dough or rolls to create a glossy finish. Bake for 25-30 minutes or until the brioche is golden brown on top and sounds hollow when tapped on the bottom.

Nutritional Info (per serving)

Calories: 250 | Fat: 15g | Carbs: 28g | Protein: 5g

Focaccia with Toppings

Ingredients

3 ½ cups all-purpose flour | 1 tablespoon instant dry yeast | 1 ½ teaspoons salt | 1 teaspoon sugar | 1 ¼ cups warm water (about 110°F) | ¼ cup extra virgin olive oil, plus more for drizzling | Fresh rosemary, for topping (optional) | Sea salt, for topping (optional) | Additional toppings of choice: cherry tomatoes, olives, caramelized onions, garlic, etc.

Preparation Time: 15 minutes

Cooking Time: 25-30 minutes & 1 hours (for rising)

Servings: 8-10 servings

Directions

1. Attach the flat beater to the stand mixer. In the mixing bowl, combine the warm water, sugar, and yeast. Stir gently to dissolve the sugar, then let it sit for 5 minutes until the mixture becomes frothy and bubbly, which indicates that the yeast is active.
2. Add the flour and salt to the yeast mixture in the stand mixer. Switch to the dough hook attachment. Mix on low speed until the dough starts to come together, then increase the speed to medium and knead for about 5-7 minutes.
3. Once the dough is kneaded, drizzle a little olive oil on the dough and around the sides of the bowl to prevent sticking. Cover the bowl with a clean kitchen towel or plastic wrap and let the dough rise in a warm spot for about 1 hour, or until it doubles in size.
4. Preheat your oven to 425°F (220°C). After the dough has risen, punch it down gently to release any air bubbles. Turn the dough out onto a lightly floured surface and stretch it out with your hands to fit a greased 9x13-inch baking pan. Alternatively, for a thicker focaccia, use a smaller pan.

5. Drizzle olive oil generously over the top of the dough, using your fingers to create dimples across the surface. Add the toppings of your choice, such as fresh rosemary, sea salt, cherry tomatoes, olives, or caramelized onions. Be creative—this is where you can personalize your focaccia.
6. Cover the pan loosely with a clean towel and let the dough rise again for about 30 minutes.
7. Place the baking pan in the preheated oven and bake for 25-30 minutes, or until the focaccia is golden brown and cooked through.

Nutritional Value (per serving)

Calories: ~200-250 kcal | Carbohydrates: 30g | Protein: 4g | Fat: 7g | Fiber: 1g | Sodium: 250mg

Honey Oatmeal Bread

Ingredients

1 cup old-fashioned rolled oats | 1 ¼ cups warm water (about 110°F/43°C) | 2 tablespoons honey | 2 tablespoons butter, softened | 2 teaspoons salt | 2 ½ teaspoons active dry yeast | 3 cups all-purpose flour | 1 tablespoon vegetable oil (for greasing the bowl) | 1 tablespoon rolled oats (for topping)

Prep Time: 15 minutes

Bake Time: 30-35 minutes

Total Time: 1 hour 50 minutes

Servings: 1 loaf (12-14 slices)

Directions

1. In a small bowl, combine the warm water and honey. Sprinkle the active dry yeast over the top of the mixture and stir gently. Allow it to sit for about 5 minutes until the yeast becomes foamy.
2. Attach the flat beater to the stand mixer. In the mixer's bowl, combine the oats, salt, and flour. Add the yeast mixture and softened butter. Mix on low speed until the ingredients begin to combine. Gradually increase the speed to medium and mix for 2-3 minutes, ensuring all ingredients are evenly incorporated.
3. Switch to the dough hook attachment. Knead the dough on medium speed for about 6-8 minutes, until the dough is smooth, elastic, and slightly sticky to the touch.
4. Lightly grease a large bowl with vegetable oil. Shape the dough into a ball and place it in the bowl, turning it once to coat it in the oil. Cover the bowl with a clean kitchen towel or plastic wrap. Allow the dough to rise in a warm place for about 1 hour or until it doubles in size.
5. After the dough has risen, punch it down gently to release any air bubbles. Transfer it to a lightly floured surface. Shape the dough into a loaf by folding in the edges and rolling it up into a tight cylinder.
6. Grease a 9x5-inch loaf pan with oil or butter. Place the shaped dough into the pan and cover it again with a kitchen towel. Let the dough rise for an additional 30-40 minutes, or until it has risen just above the edges of the pan.
7. While the dough is undergoing its second rise, preheat your oven to 375°F (190°C).
8. Once the dough has risen sufficiently, sprinkle the top with rolled oats for a nice rustic touch. Bake the loaf for 30-35 minutes. If the top starts to brown too quickly, you can loosely cover it with aluminum foil.

Nutritional Value (per serving, 1 slice)

Calories: ~120 | Carbohydrates: 24g | Protein: 3g | Fat: 2g | Fiber: 2g | Sugar: 6g | Sodium: 180mg

A short message from the author

Hey there! How's the book treating you? I'm super curious to know what you think about it! Your thoughts can really make a difference.

Could you spare just a minute to jot down a quick review on Amazon? Even a few sentences would mean the world!

Simply click the link 🔗 or scan the QR code below and scroll down to get to the *'Write a customer review'* button to leave your review on Amazon

🔗 rebrand.ly/stand/mixer/lm

QR code

Thank you for taking the time to share your thoughts!

PASTA

15. Ricotta Tortellini
16. Spinach Pasta Dough
17. Cheese Ravioli
18. Veggie Noodles
19. Fettuccine Alfredo
20. Squid Ink Pasta
21. Whole Wheat Pasta Dough
22. Gluten-Free Pasta Dough
23. Beetroot Pasta Dough
24. Pappardelle Bolognese
25. Lasagna Sheets
26. Sweet Potato Gnocchi
27. Pasta Carbonara

Ricotta Tortellini

Ingredients

For the Pasta Dough: 2 cups all-purpose flour (plus extra for dusting) | 3 large eggs | 1 tablespoon olive oil | ½ teaspoon salt

For the Ricotta Filling: 1 cup ricotta cheese (drained) | ¼ cup freshly grated Parmesan cheese | 1 egg yolk | ¼ teaspoon ground nutmeg | Salt and freshly ground black pepper, to taste

Prep Time: 30 minutes

Resting Time (for dough): 30 minutes

Cook Time: 3-4 minutes per batch

Servings: About 24 pieces of tortellini (depending on size)

Directions

1. Attach the flat beater to your stand mixer. In the mixing bowl, combine the flour and salt. Make a well in the center and crack in the eggs and olive oil. Start mixing on low speed (Speed 2) until the dough begins to come together.
2. Once it starts to form, switch to the dough hook attachment. Knead the dough on medium speed for about 5-7 minutes. The dough should be smooth and elastic, but slightly firm. If it's too sticky, add a little more flour, one tablespoon at a time. Once kneaded, wrap the dough in plastic wrap and let it rest for 30 minutes at room temperature.
3. Prepare the Ricotta Filling: Mix the ricotta cheese, Parmesan cheese, egg yolk, nutmeg, salt, and pepper. Stir until the mixture is smooth and well-combined. Set it aside.
4. Once the dough has rested, divide it into 4 equal parts. Roll out the dough using the KitchenAid pasta roller attachment. Start on the thickest setting and gradually work your way to thinner settings

(about 2-3 on the dial) to get a nice, thin sheet of pasta. Dust with flour as needed to prevent sticking.

5. Lay the pasta sheet on a flat surface, dusted with flour. Using a round cutter (about 3 inches in diameter), cut out circles of dough. Place a small teaspoon of the ricotta filling in the center of each dough circle.
6. Fold the circle in half to form a half-moon shape, pinching the edges together to seal the filling inside. Bring the two corners of the half-moon together to form the traditional tortellini shape. Press the edges firmly to ensure they stay sealed.
7. Bring a large pot of salted water to a boil. Gently drop the tortellini into the boiling water. Cook for 3-4 minutes, or until the tortellini float to the surface. Remove with a slotted spoon and transfer to a plate.
8. Serve the tortellini with your favorite sauce, a rich butter sage sauce, a tomato sauce, or a creamy Alfredo. Optionally, garnish with more grated Parmesan cheese and fresh herbs like basil.

Nutritional Value (per serving, 4 pieces)

Calories: ~180 | Carbohydrates: 25g | Protein: 8g | Fat: 7g | Fiber: 2g | Sugar: 2g | Sodium: 250mg

Tip: If you're making a larger batch, you can freeze the uncooked tortellini on a baking sheet and transfer them to a ziplock bag once frozen for easy storage.

Spinach Pasta Dough

Ingredients

2 cups all-purpose flour | 2 large eggs | 1 cup fresh spinach leaves | 1 tablespoon olive oil | 1 teaspoon salt | Water, as needed (about 1-2 tablespoons)

Prep Time: 15 minutes

Resting Time (for dough to rest): 30 minutes

Total Time: 50 minutes

Servings: Enough dough for about 2 servings of pasta

Directions

1. Prepare the Spinach Puree: Begin by blanching the spinach. In a small pot of boiling water, cook the spinach leaves for 1-2 minutes, just until wilted. Drain the spinach and run it under cold water to stop the cooking process. Gently squeeze out excess water from the spinach, then place the leaves in a blender or food processor. Puree until smooth, set aside.
2. Attach the flat beater to your stand mixer. In the mixing bowl, add the flour and salt. Turn the mixer on low speed to gently combine. Then, add the eggs and spinach puree. Mix on low speed until the dough starts coming together. Add the olive oil and mix until fully incorporated.
3. Switch to the dough hook attachment. Knead the dough on medium speed for 6-8 minutes. If the dough feels too dry, add a small amount of water (1-2 tablespoons at a time) until the dough comes together and forms a smooth, elastic ball. If it's too sticky, sprinkle in a little extra flour.
4. Once the dough is smooth and elastic, cover it with a damp towel or plastic wrap. Allow the dough to rest for 30 minutes at room temperature.
5. After the dough has rested, divide it into smaller portions for easier handling. Using the pasta roller attachment, set it to the widest setting (usually #1). Flatten a portion of the dough into a rough rectangle and feed it through the pasta roller. Fold the dough in half and roll it through again. Repeat this process 3-4 times to knead the dough further and get a smooth, elastic sheet.
6. Gradually reduce the roller's setting (moving to a lower number) to progressively thin the dough to your desired thickness, usually around setting #4 or #5 for most pasta types.
7. After the dough is rolled out to the desired thickness, switch to the pasta cutter attachment (e.g., fettuccine, tagliatelle, or spaghetti cutter). Feed the dough sheet through the cutter, and fresh pasta strands will emerge ready to be cooked.
8. Fresh pasta cooks quickly, so bring a large pot of salted water to a boil. Cook the spinach pasta for about 2-3 minutes until al dente, then drain and serve with your favorite sauce.

Nutritional Value (per serving)

Calories: ~200 | Carbohydrates: 40g | Protein: 8g | Fat: 4g | Fiber: 3g | Sugar: 1g | Sodium: 200mg

Cheese Ravioli

Ingredients

For the Pasta Dough: 2 cups all-purpose flour | 2 large eggs | 1 tablespoon olive oil | 1 teaspoon salt | 2-3 tablespoons water (as needed)

For the Cheese Filling: 1 ½ cups ricotta cheese (drained) | 1 cup shredded mozzarella cheese | ¼ cup grated Parmesan cheese |1 egg yolk | 1 tablespoon chopped fresh basil (optional) | Salt and pepper, to taste

Prep Time: 20 minutes

Total Time: 1 hour 30 minutes

Servings: Approximately 24 ravioli

Directions

1. Attach the flat beater to the stand mixer. In the mixer's bowl, add the flour and salt. Add the eggs and olive oil to the bowl. Mix on low speed until the dough starts to come together, about 2 minutes.
2. Switch to the dough hook attachment. Gradually add 2 tablespoons of water and knead on medium speed for 5-7 minutes, or until the dough is smooth and elastic. If needed, add additional water (1 tablespoon at a time) to bring the dough together. The dough should be slightly tacky but not sticky.
3. Form the dough into a ball and wrap it in plastic wrap. Let it rest at room temperature for at least 30 minutes.
4. Prepare the Cheese Filling: In a bowl, mix the ricotta, mozzarella, and Parmesan cheeses. Add the egg yolk, basil (if using), and season with salt and pepper to taste. Stir well to combine until you have a creamy, well-blended filling.
5. After the dough has rested, divide it into 4 pieces. Work with one piece at a time and keep the others wrapped to prevent them from drying out. Attach the pasta roller attachment to the stand

mixer. Begin by rolling the dough through the roller at the widest setting. Fold the dough into thirds and pass it through the roller again, repeating this process about 3-4 times until the dough is smooth and elastic.

6. Gradually narrow the roller setting until you reach the desired thickness (usually setting 4-5 on the KitchenAid roller). The dough should be thin but not tearing.
7. Once the dough is rolled out, place one sheet of pasta on a clean, lightly floured surface. Using a spoon, drop small mounds of the cheese filling (about 1 teaspoon each) onto the pasta, spaced 1 inch apart. Brush the edges of the pasta sheet with a small amount of water, then place a second sheet of pasta over the top.
8. Press around each mound of filling to seal the ravioli, ensuring there are no air pockets inside. Use a ravioli cutter or a sharp knife to cut between each mound of filling, forming individual ravioli. Press the edges with a fork to seal them tightly.
9. Cook the Ravioli: Bring a large pot of salted water to a boil. Carefully drop the ravioli into the boiling water, a few at a time, making sure not to overcrowd the pot. Cook for 4-5 minutes, or until the ravioli float to the surface.
10. Serve your cheese ravioli with your favorite sauce—marinara, pesto, or a simple butter and sage sauce. Garnish with freshly grated Parmesan cheese and a sprinkle of basil, if desired.

Nutritional Value (per serving, 3 ravioli)

Calories: ~120 | Carbohydrates: 18g | Protein: 6g | Fat: 5g | Fiber: 1g | Sugar: 1g | Sodium: 180mg

Veggie Noodles

Ingredients

2 ½ cups all-purpose flour (plus extra for dusting)| 3 large eggs | 2 tablespoons vegetable puree (spinach, beetroot, or carrot) | 1 tablespoon olive oil | ½ teaspoon salt

Prep Time: 20 minutes

Resting Time: 30 minutes | **Cooking Time**: 3-5 minutes

Total Time: 55 minutes

Servings: 4

Directions

1. Steam or boil your chosen vegetable (e.g., spinach, carrots, or beets) until tender. Blend the cooked vegetable in a food processor until smooth, and let it cool to room temperature.
2. Attach the flat beater to your stand mixer. In the mixer's bowl, combine the flour and salt. Create a small well in the center and add the eggs, vegetable puree, and olive oil. Mix on low speed until the ingredients begin to come together. Increase to medium speed and mix for 2-3 minutes until the dough starts to form.
3. Switch to the dough hook attachment. Knead the dough on medium speed for about 6-8 minutes until it becomes smooth, elastic, and slightly firm. If the dough feels too sticky, add a small amount of flour, one tablespoon at a time. If it's too dry, add a few drops of water.
4. Wrap the dough tightly in plastic wrap and let it rest at room temperature for at least 30 minutes.
5. Attach the KitchenAid Pasta Roller to the stand mixer. Divide the dough into four equal portions, keeping unused portions covered to prevent drying. Flatten one portion slightly and pass it through the widest setting of the pasta roller. Fold it in half and repeat several times to create a smooth, uniform sheet. Gradually adjust the roller to thinner settings until the desired thickness is achieved.
6. Switch to the KitchenAid Pasta Cutter attachment (e.g., for fettuccine or spaghetti) to cut the sheets into noodles. Dust the noodles lightly with flour to prevent sticking.
7. Cook the Noodles: Bring a large pot of salted water to a boil. Cook the veggie noodles for 3-5 minutes, depending on their thickness, until al dente. Drain and toss with your favorite sauce or toppings.

Nutritional Value (per serving)

Calories: ~210 | Carbohydrates: 38g | Protein: 7g | Fat: 4g | Fiber: 3g | Sodium: 150mg

Fettuccine Alfredo

Ingredients

For the Fettuccine (Fresh Pasta Dough): 2 cups all-purpose flour | 3 large eggs | ½ teaspoon salt | 1 tablespoon olive oil

For the Alfredo Sauce: 2 tablespoons unsalted butter | 1 cup heavy cream | 1 cup grated Parmesan cheese| Salt and freshly ground black pepper to taste | Fresh parsley, chopped (for garnish)

Prep Time: 20 minutes

Total Time: 1 hour

Servings: 4 servings

Directions

1. Attach the flat beater to the stand mixer. Add the flour and salt to the mixer bowl and mix on low speed to combine. Crack the eggs into a small bowl and lightly beat them with a fork. Slowly add the eggs and olive oil to the flour mixture while the mixer runs on low speed.
2. Once the dough starts coming together, switch to the dough hook attachment. Knead on medium speed for about 5-7 minutes until the dough is smooth and elastic. If the dough is too sticky, add a little more flour (1 tablespoon at a time). If it's too dry, add a small amount of water.
3. Shape the dough into a ball, wrap it in plastic wrap, and let it rest at room temperature for 30 minutes. This allows the gluten to relax, making it easier to roll out.
4. Attach the pasta roller attachment to the stand mixer. Divide the dough into four portions and flatten each into a rectangular shape. Starting on the widest setting, feed one portion of dough through the roller. Fold it in half and roll again. Repeat this process, gradually narrowing the roller setting, until the dough is thin (usually setting 5 or 6).

5. Switch to the fettuccine cutter attachment and feed the rolled-out dough through it to create fettuccine strands. Lightly dust the strands with flour to prevent sticking. Repeat with the remaining portions of dough.
6. Cooking the Pasta: Bring a large pot of salted water to a boil. Cook the fettuccine for 2-3 minutes until al dente. Fresh pasta cooks much faster than dried pasta. Reserve ½ cup of pasta water before draining.
7. Making the Alfredo Sauce: In a large skillet, melt the butter over medium heat. Stir in the heavy cream and simmer gently for 2-3 minutes. Gradually add the grated Parmesan cheese, stirring constantly, until the cheese melts and the sauce thickens. If the sauce is too thick, add a splash of the reserved pasta water. Season with salt and freshly ground black pepper to taste.
8. Add the cooked fettuccine to the skillet with the sauce. Toss gently to coat the pasta evenly with the Alfredo sauce. Garnish with fresh parsley and additional Parmesan cheese if desired.

Nutritional Value (per serving)

Calories: ~450 | Carbohydrates: 40g | Protein: 14g | Fat: 25g | Sodium: 400mg

Tips:

- ✓ For added protein, sauté chicken or shrimp and toss it into the Alfredo sauce before serving.
- ✓ If you prefer a lighter sauce, substitute half of the heavy cream with whole milk.
- ✓ Ensure the Parmesan cheese is freshly grated to prevent clumping in the sauce.

Ingredients

2 cups (250g) all-purpose flour | 2 large eggs | 1 tablespoon squid ink (available in specialty stores or online) | ½ teaspoon salt | 1 tablespoon olive oil | Extra flour for dusting

Prep Time: 20 minutes

Total Time: 55 minutes

Servings: 4

Directions

1. Attach the flat beater to your stand mixer. In the mixer's bowl, combine the flour and salt. In a small bowl, whisk together the eggs, squid ink, and olive oil until smooth. Gradually add the wet ingredients to the flour mixture with the mixer running on low speed.
2. Once the ingredients are mostly combined, switch to the dough hook attachment. Knead the dough on medium speed for about 8-10 minutes, or until it forms a smooth, elastic ball. If the dough is too sticky, add a little more flour, one tablespoon at a time. If it's too dry, add a small amount of water.
3. Wrap the dough in plastic wrap or cover it with a damp kitchen towel. Let it rest at room temperature for at least 30 minutes.
4. Attach the pasta roller attachment to your stand mixer. Divide the dough into 4 pieces. Flatten one piece into a small rectangle, keeping the remaining dough covered to prevent it from drying out. Run the dough through the widest setting (typically setting 1) on the pasta roller. Fold it in half and repeat this step 2-3 times.
5. Gradually decrease the thickness setting, one notch at a time, until the dough reaches your desired thinness (setting 5 or 6 works well for squid ink pasta). Dust the dough lightly with flour if it becomes sticky. Repeat this process with the remaining dough pieces.
6. Switch to the fettuccine or spaghetti cutter attachment (depending on your preference) and feed the rolled-out dough through the cutter. Lightly toss the cut pasta with flour to prevent it from sticking together.
7. Cook the Pasta: Bring a large pot of salted water to a boil. Add the pasta and cook for 2-3 minutes, or until it's al dente. Fresh pasta cooks much faster than dried pasta, so keep an eye on it.
8. Serve: Drain the pasta and serve immediately with your sauce of choice. Squid ink pasta pairs beautifully with a seafood sauce, garlic and olive oil, or a light cream sauce.

Nutritional Value (per serving)

Calories: ~220 | Carbohydrates: 36g | Protein: 8g | Fat: 4g | Fiber: 1g | Sodium: 80mg

Tips: Squid ink can stain surfaces, so use gloves and clean your tools promptly after use.

Whole Wheat Pasta Dough

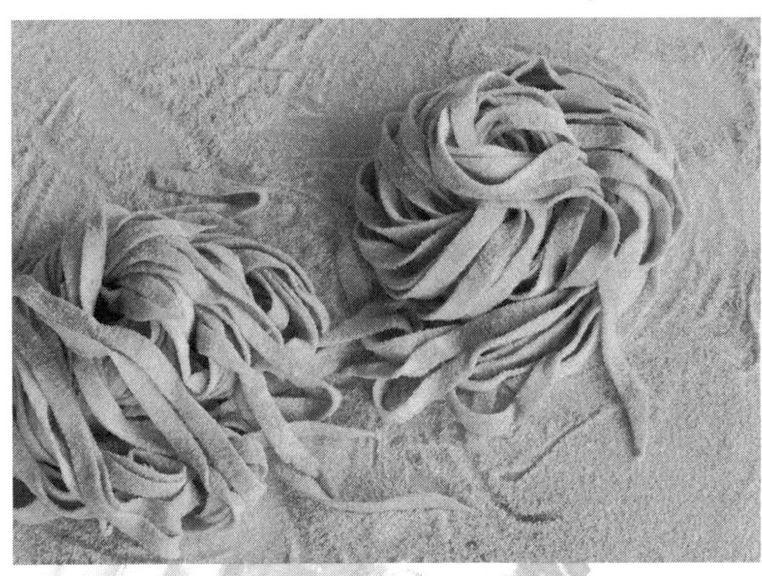

Ingredients

1 ½ cups whole wheat flour | 1 cup all-purpose flour (for better elasticity) | 3 large eggs | 1 tablespoon olive oil | 1-2 teaspoons water (if needed) | ½ teaspoon salt

Servings: 3 (depending on pasta shape)

Directions

Follow the same steps as the **Lemon Herb Pasta Dough**, substituting the flours. Note that whole wheat dough may require slightly more water to reach the right consistency. Knead a bit longer (10-12 minutes) for a smooth dough, as whole wheat flour is denser.

Nutritional Information (per serving)

Calories: ~240 | Carbohydrates: 42g | Protein: 9g | Fat: 5g | Fiber: 6g | Sodium: 120mg

Tip: Whole wheat pasta pairs well with robust sauces, such as marinara or mushroom ragu.

Gluten-Free Pasta Dough

Ingredients

2 cups gluten-free all-purpose flour blend (ensure it contains xanthan gum or guar gum for structure) | 1 teaspoon psyllium husk powder (optional, for elasticity) | 3 large eggs | 1 tablespoon olive oil | 1 tablespoon water (as needed) | ½ teaspoon salt

Servings: 4

Directions

Follow the same steps as the **Lemon Herb Pasta Dough**, substituting the flours.

Nutritional Information (per serving)

Calories: ~230 | Carbohydrates: 40g | Protein: 7g | Fat: 5g | Fiber: 2g | Sodium: 120mg

Tips: Pair with light sauces, such as garlic butter or pesto, to let the flavor of the pasta shine.

Beetroot Pasta Dough

Ingredients

1 medium beetroot, cooked and pureed (about ½ cup beet puree) | 2 cups all-purpose flour (plus extra for dusting) | 2 large eggs | 1 tablespoon olive oil | ½ teaspoon salt

Servings: 4 (depending on pasta shape)

Directions

Follow the same steps as the **Lemon Herb Pasta Dough**, add the beetroot.

Nutritional Value (per serving)

Calories: ~150 | Carbohydrates: 30g | Protein: 5g | Fat: 2g | Fiber: 2g | Sugar: 3g | Sodium: 180mg

Pappardelle Bolognese

Ingredients

For the Pasta: 2 ½ cups all-purpose flour (plus extra for dusting) | 4 large eggs | ½ teaspoon salt | 1 tablespoon olive oil (optional)

For the Bolognese Sauce: 2 tablespoons olive oil | 1 medium onion, finely chopped | 1 carrot, finely diced | 1 celery stalk, finely diced | 3 cloves garlic, minced | 1 pound ground beef (or a mix of beef and pork) | 1 cup whole milk | ½ cup dry white wine | 1 (14-ounce) can crushed tomatoes | 1 teaspoon dried oregano | Salt and pepper, to taste | Freshly grated Parmesan cheese, for serving | Fresh basil leaves, for garnish

Prep Time: 40 minutes

Total Time: 2 hours 40 minutes

Servings: 4

Directions

1. Attach the flat beater to your stand mixer. In the mixing bowl, add the flour and salt. Crack the eggs into the center of the flour, and optionally add olive oil for a silkier texture. Mix on low speed until the dough begins to form.
2. Replace the flat beater with the dough hook attachment. Knead the dough on low speed for about 8-10 minutes until it becomes smooth, elastic, and slightly tacky.
3. Shape the dough into a ball, wrap it tightly in plastic wrap, and let it rest for 30 minutes at room temperature.
4. Attach the pasta roller attachment to your stand mixer. Divide the rested dough into four pieces. Flatten one piece and pass it through the roller on the widest setting. Fold it in half and repeat 2-3

times to create a smooth sheet. Gradually adjust to thinner settings, rolling until the sheet is about 1/16 inch thick.

5. Lay the pasta sheet on a lightly floured surface. Using a knife or pizza cutter, cut the sheet into ¾-inch-wide ribbons to make pappardelle. Dust with flour to prevent sticking and set aside.
6. Make the Bolognese Sauce: Heat olive oil in a large skillet over medium heat. Add onion, carrot, and celery, and sauté until softened, about 5 minutes. Add garlic and cook for 1 minute. Increase the heat to medium-high and add the ground meat. Cook until browned, breaking it up with a wooden spoon as it cooks.
7. Stir in the milk and cook until it evaporates. Add the white wine and let it simmer until reduced by half. Add the crushed tomatoes and oregano, then season with salt and pepper. Lower the heat and let the sauce simmer gently for 1 ½ to 2 hours, stirring occasionally. Adjust seasoning as needed.
8. Cook the Pasta: Bring a large pot of salted water to a boil. Cook the pappardelle for 2-3 minutes until al dente. Fresh pasta cooks much faster than dried pasta.
9. Drain the pasta, reserving ½ cup of the pasta water. Toss the pappardelle with the Bolognese sauce in a large skillet over low heat. Add reserved pasta water as needed to loosen the sauce.
10. Divide the pasta among plates, top with freshly grated Parmesan cheese, and garnish with basil leaves.

Tip: For a richer flavor, prepare the sauce a day ahead and reheat before serving—it tastes even better as the flavors meld overnight.

Nutritional Value (per serving)

Calories: ~530 | Carbohydrates: 52g | Protein: 25g | Fat: 20g | Fiber: 4g | Sodium: 580mg

Lasagna Sheets

Ingredients

2 cups (250g) all-purpose flour or "00" flour (for a smoother texture) | 3 large eggs | 1 tablespoon olive oil | 1 teaspoon salt

Prep Time: 15 minutes

Total Time: 1 hour 10 minutes

Servings: Makes 12-15 lasagna sheets (suitable for a 9x13-inch lasagna dish).

Directions

1. Attach the flat beater to the stand mixer. In the mixer bowl, combine the flour and salt. Add the eggs and olive oil. Mix on low speed until the dough starts to come together, forming a shaggy texture.
2. Switch to the dough hook and knead on medium speed for 8-10 minutes, until the dough is smooth, elastic, and slightly firm.
3. Remove the dough from the bowl and shape it into a ball. Wrap it in plastic wrap and let it rest at room temperature for at least 30 minutes.
4. Attach the Pasta Roller attachment to your stand mixer. Set the roller to the widest setting (usually marked as "1"). Divide the dough into four portions. Flatten one portion slightly with your hands, keeping the remaining portions covered to prevent drying.
5. Feed the flattened dough through the pasta roller on the widest setting. Fold it in half and roll it through again. Repeat this process 2-3 times to create a smooth and even texture. Gradually reduce the roller setting to thinner levels (setting "4" or "5") until the desired thickness for lasagna sheets is achieved.
6. Lay the rolled-out pasta on a lightly floured surface. Cut it into 10-inch-long sheets to fit a standard lasagna dish. Dust each sheet with a small amount of flour to prevent sticking.
7. If using immediately, parboil the sheets for 30 seconds in salted water, then transfer them to an ice bath to stop cooking. Pat dry before assembling the lasagna. For later use, let the sheets dry completely on a clean towel or pasta drying rack before storing them in an airtight container.

Nutritional Value (per lasagna sheet)

Calories: ~70 | Carbohydrates: 10g | Protein: 3g| Fat: 2g | Sodium: 70mg

Sweet Potato Gnocchi

Ingredients

2 medium sweet potatoes | 1 ½ cups all-purpose flour (plus extra for dusting) | 1 large egg | 1 teaspoon salt | ¼ teaspoon nutmeg (optional) | 1 tablespoon olive oil (for cooking, optional)

Prep Time: 20 minutes

Total Time: 1 hour

Servings: Approximately 4

Directions

1. Begin by cooking the sweet potatoes. You can either bake or boil them. To bake, preheat your oven to 400°F (200°C), prick the sweet potatoes with a fork, and bake them on a sheet pan for 45-60 minutes until tender. For boiling, peel the sweet potatoes and cut them into chunks, then boil for 15-20 minutes until soft. Mash the potato.
2. Attach the flat beater to your stand mixer. In the mixer bowl, add the cooked sweet potato (mashed) and the egg. Mix on low speed until well combined. Gradually add the flour, salt, and optional nutmeg to the sweet potato mixture. Mix on low speed until the ingredients come together into a dough.
3. Once combined, switch to the dough hook attachment and knead on medium speed for 3-4 minutes until the dough is smooth and slightly sticky but not overly wet.
4. Remove the dough from the mixer and place it on a lightly floured surface. Cover with a clean kitchen towel and let it rest for 15-30 minutes.
5. After the dough has rested, divide it into 4 portions. Using the pasta roller attachment, roll each portion into a long rope, about 1-inch thick. Using a knife or dough scraper, cut the ropes into 1-inch

pieces. For traditional gnocchi, gently press each piece with a fork to create ridges that help the sauce cling to the gnocchi.

6. Cook the Gnocchi: Bring a large pot of salted water to a boil. Drop the gnocchi into the boiling water in batches. They are ready when they float to the top, typically within 2-3 minutes.
7. Finish and Serve: For added flavor, you can sauté the cooked gnocchi in a bit of olive oil or butter for a crispy texture on the outside. Serve with your favorite sauce, such as brown butter with sage, marinara, or even a simple garlic and olive oil drizzle.

Nutritional Value (per serving, ¼ of recipe)

Calories: ~200 | Carbohydrates: 45g | Protein: 3g | Fat: 1g | Fiber: 3g | Sugar: 6g | Sodium: 300mg

Pasta Carbonara

Ingredients

For the Pasta Dough: 2 cups all-purpose flour (plus extra for dusting) | 2 large eggs | 1 tablespoon olive oil | 1 teaspoon salt

For the Carbonara Sauce: 8 oz pancetta or guanciale, diced | 2 large eggs | 1 cup Parmesan cheese, freshly grated | 1 cup Pecorino Romano cheese, freshly grated | Freshly ground black pepper, to taste | 2 tablespoons pasta cooking water (reserved from the cooked pasta) | Salt, to taste

Prep Time (for dough): 10 minutes

Cook Time (for pasta and sauce): 15-20 minutes

Servings: 4

Directions

1. In the bowl of your stand mixer, combine the flour and salt. Attach the pasta dough hook to the mixer. Make a well in the center of the flour mixture and add the eggs and olive oil.
2. Start mixing on low speed to combine the ingredients. As the dough begins to form, increase the speed to medium and let the mixer knead the dough for about 5 minutes until it becomes smooth and elastic.
3. Once kneaded, wrap the dough in plastic wrap and let it rest for 30 minutes at room temperature.
4. After the dough has rested, divide it into 4 equal portions. Attach the pasta roller attachment to your stand mixer. Flatten one portion of dough into a rough rectangle and feed it through the roller, starting on the widest setting.
5. Fold the dough into thirds and roll it again, gradually reducing the thickness of the roller setting until the dough is about 1/8-inch thick. Dust the rolled-out dough lightly with flour to prevent sticking and cut it into fettuccine or tagliatelle using the appropriate pasta cutter attachment.
6. Cook the Pasta: Bring a large pot of salted water to a boil. Add the fresh pasta and cook for 2-3 minutes, or until al dente. Fresh pasta cooks much faster than dried pasta, so keep an eye on it! Drain the pasta, reserving ½ cup of the pasta water
7. Make the Carbonara Sauce: While the pasta is cooking, heat a large skillet over medium heat. Add the diced pancetta or guanciale and cook until crispy and golden brown, about 5-7 minutes. In a bowl, whisk together the eggs, grated Parmesan, Pecorino Romano, and freshly ground black pepper. Set aside.
8. Combine the Pasta and Sauce: Add the cooked pasta to the skillet with the pancetta, tossing to combine. Remove the skillet from heat and immediately pour in the egg and cheese mixture, tossing quickly to avoid scrambling the eggs. Add reserved pasta cooking water a little at a time to adjust the sauce's consistency. Taste and adjust seasoning with salt and additional pepper, if needed.

Nutritional Value (per serving)

Calories: ~500 | Carbohydrates: 60g | Protein: 22g | Fat: 22g | Fiber: 2g | Sugar: 2g | Sodium: 850mg

Tips:

- ✓ You can add a tablespoon of heavy cream to the sauce mixture, though traditional Carbonara is made without cream.
- ✓ If you can find it, use guanciale (cured pork cheek) instead of pancetta for a more authentic taste.

CAKES

28. Orange Chiffon Cake

29. Classic Vanilla Sponge Cake

30. Chocolate Fudge Cake

31. Carrot Cake with Cream Cheese Frosting

32. Red Velvet Cake

33. Lemon Pound Cake

34. Angel Food Cake

35. Tres Leches Cake

36. Hummingbird Cake

37. Coconut Layer Cake

38. Funfetti Cake

39. Black Forest Cake

40. Cheesecake

Orange Chiffon Cake

Ingredients

For the Cake Batter: 2 ¼ cups all-purpose flour | 1 ½ cups granulated sugar | 1 tablespoon baking powder | ½ teaspoon salt | 7 large eggs, separated | ¾ cup vegetable oil | ¾ cup freshly squeezed orange juice | 1 tablespoon orange zest | 1 teaspoon vanilla extract | ½ teaspoon cream of tartar

For the Orange Glaze (optional): 1 cup powdered sugar | 2 tablespoons freshly squeezed orange juice | 1 teaspoon orange zest

Prep Time: 15 minutes

Cook Time: 55-60 minutes

Servings: 12

Directions

1. Preheat your oven to 325°F (163°C). Do not grease the pan. Use an angel food cake pan or a tube pan, which will allow the batter to rise properly and create the signature airy texture of chiffon cakes.
2. Prepare the Dry Ingredients: In the mixing bowl of your stand mixer, combine the flour, sugar, baking powder, and salt. Use the flat beater attachment on a low speed to mix the dry ingredients together until fully combined.
3. In a separate bowl, whisk together the egg yolks, vegetable oil, orange juice, orange zest, and vanilla extract. Add this mixture to the dry ingredients in your stand mixer bowl. Use the flat beater attachment to mix on low speed until everything is fully incorporated, forming a smooth batter. Scrape down the sides of the bowl as necessary to ensure everything is evenly mixed.

4. Attach the whisk attachment to your stand mixer. In a clean, dry bowl, add the egg whites and the cream of tartar. Beat on medium-high speed until soft peaks form. This should take about 2-3 minutes. Once soft peaks form, continue to whip until stiff peaks form.
5. Carefully fold the whipped egg whites into the batter. Start by adding a small amount of egg whites to lighten the mixture, and then gently fold in the rest using a spatula.
6. Bake the Cake: Pour the batter into the ungreased tube pan. Smooth the top with a spatula. Bake the cake in the preheated oven for about 55-60 minutes, or until a toothpick inserted into the center comes out clean.
7. Once baked, remove the cake from the oven and invert the pan onto a cooling rack (if using an angel food cake pan with legs, simply place it upside down). Allow the cake to cool completely in the pan.
8. Glaze (Optional): If you'd like to add a glaze, whisk together powdered sugar, orange juice, and orange zest in a small bowl until smooth. Drizzle the glaze over the cooled cake.

Nutritional Value (per serving)

Calories: ~220 | Carbohydrates: 38g | Protein: 4g | Fat: 8g | Fiber: 0g | Sugar: 19g | Sodium: 150mg

Classic Vanilla Sponge Cake

Ingredients

For the Cake: 1 cup (2 sticks) unsalted butter, softened | 2 cups granulated sugar | 4 large eggs, room temperature | 2 ½ cups all-purpose flour | 2 ½ teaspoons baking powder | ½ teaspoon salt | 1 cup whole milk, room temperature | 2 teaspoons pure vanilla extract

For Frosting (optional): 1 cup unsalted butter, softened | 4 cups powdered sugar | 2-4 tablespoons milk | 2 teaspoons vanilla extract

Prep Time: 20 minutes

Total Time: ~55 minutes

Servings: 2 9-inch cake layers

Directions

1. Preheat your oven to 350°F (175°C). Grease and flour two 9-inch round cake pans or line them with parchment paper for easy removal.
2. Attach the flat beater to your stand mixer. In the bowl of your stand mixer, add the softened butter and sugar. Beat on medium speed until the mixture is light and fluffy, about 3-4 minutes. Scrape down the sides of the bowl as needed.
3. Reduce the mixer speed to low and add the eggs one at a time, ensuring each egg is fully incorporated before adding the next. Add the vanilla extract and mix until combined.
4. Mix Dry Ingredients: In a separate bowl, whisk together the all-purpose flour, baking powder, and salt. With the mixer on low speed, gradually add the dry ingredients to the butter mixture, alternating with the milk. Start and end with the dry ingredients (e.g., dry, milk, dry).
5. Divide the batter evenly between the prepared cake pans, smoothing the tops with a spatula. Gently tap the pans on the counter to release any air bubbles.
6. Bake the Cakes: Place the pans on the center rack of the preheated oven. Bake for 30-35 minutes or until a toothpick inserted into the center comes out clean.
7. Prepare the Frosting (Optional): Clean the stand mixer bowl and attach the paddle attachment. Add the softened butter to the bowl and beat on medium speed until creamy. Gradually add the powdered sugar, one cup at a time, mixing on low speed until incorporated. Add vanilla extract and milk, 1 tablespoon at a time, until the frosting reaches the desired consistency.
8. Once the cake layers are fully cooled, place one layer on a serving plate. Spread an even layer of frosting on top. Place the second layer on top and frost the top and sides of the cake. Decorate as desired.

Nutritional Value (per serving)

Calories: ~350 | Carbohydrates: 52g | Protein: 5g | Fat: 14g | Fiber: 1g | Sugar: 38g | Sodium: 150mg

Chocolate Fudge Cake

Ingredients

For the Cake: 1 ¾ cups all-purpose flour | ¾ cup unsweetened cocoa powder | 1 ½ teaspoons baking powder | 1 ½ teaspoons baking soda | 1 teaspoon salt | 2 cups granulated sugar | 2 large eggs | 1 cup whole milk | ½ cup vegetable oil | 2 teaspoons vanilla extract | 1 cup boiling water

For the Fudge Frosting: 1 cup unsalted butter, softened | 3 ½ cups powdered sugar | ½ cup unsweetened cocoa powder| 1 teaspoon vanilla extract | ¼ cup heavy cream

Prep Time: 20 minutes

Total Time: ~2 hours

Servings: 12

Directions

1. Preheat the oven to 350°F (175°C). Grease and flour two 9-inch round cake pans or line them with parchment paper.
2. In the bowl of your stand mixer, combine the flour, cocoa powder, baking powder, baking soda, salt, and sugar using the paddle attachment. Mix on low speed until evenly combined.
3. Add the eggs, milk, oil, and vanilla extract to the dry ingredients. Beat on medium speed for 2-3 minutes until the batter is smooth and glossy. Reduce the mixer speed to low and gradually pour in the boiling water. The batter will be thin, but this step ensures a moist cake.
4. Divide the batter evenly between the prepared pans. Tap the pans gently on the counter to release any air bubbles. Bake in the preheated oven for 30-35 minutes or until a toothpick inserted in the center comes out clean.

5. Prepare the Fudge Frosting: In the cleaned bowl of your stand mixer, cream the softened butter using the paddle attachment on medium speed until light and fluffy, about 2 minutes. Sift together the powdered sugar and cocoa powder to remove any lumps. Gradually add this mixture to the butter on low speed, mixing until combined. Add the vanilla extract and heavy cream. Increase the mixer speed to medium-high and beat for 2-3 minutes until the frosting is smooth and creamy. Adjust the consistency with more cream if needed.
6. Assemble the Cake: Place one cake layer on a serving plate. Spread an even layer of frosting on top. Add the second cake layer and frost the top and sides of the cake. Use an offset spatula for a smooth finish.
7. Decorate and Serve: Garnish with chocolate shavings, sprinkles, or fresh berries, if desired.

Nutritional Value (per serving)

Calories: ~430 | Carbohydrates: 58g | Protein: 5g | Fat: 20g | Fiber: 3g | Sugar: 45g | Sodium: 290mg

Carrot Cake with Cream Cheese Frosting

Ingredients

For the Cake: 2 cups all-purpose flour | 1 ½ teaspoons baking powder | 1 teaspoon baking soda | 1 teaspoon ground cinnamon | ½ teaspoon ground nutmeg | ½ teaspoon ground ginger | ½ teaspoon salt | 1 cup granulated sugar | ½ cup brown sugar | ¾ cup vegetable oil | 4 large eggs | 1 teaspoon vanilla extract | 2 cups grated carrots | 1 cup chopped walnuts or pecans (optional) | ½ cup crushed pineapple, drained (optional)

For the Cream Cheese Frosting: 8 oz cream cheese, softened | ½ cup unsalted butter, softened | 3 cups powdered sugar | 1 teaspoon vanilla extract

Prep Time: 15 minutes

Cook Time: 35-40 minutes

Servings: 12

Directions

1. Preheat your oven to 350°F (175°C). Grease and flour two 9-inch round cake pans or line them with parchment paper. Attach the paddle attachment to your stand mixer. In the mixing bowl, combine the granulated sugar, brown sugar, and vegetable oil. Start on low speed, gradually increasing to medium speed, and mix until well combined and smooth. Add the eggs one at a time, followed by the vanilla extract. Mix on medium speed until fully incorporated.
2. In a separate bowl, whisk together the flour, baking powder, baking soda, cinnamon, nutmeg, ginger, and salt. Reduce the stand mixer speed to low and gradually add the dry ingredients to the wet mixture, mixing just until combined. Add the grated carrots, nuts, and pineapple (if using). Mix on low speed until evenly distributed throughout the batter.
3. Divide the batter evenly between the prepared cake pans and smooth the tops with a spatula. Bake in the preheated oven for 35-40 minutes, or until a toothpick inserted into the center comes out clean. Remove the cakes from the oven and let them cool in the pans for 10 minutes.
4. Prepare the Cream Cheese Frosting: Clean the mixing bowl and attach the paddle attachment. Add the softened cream cheese and butter to the bowl. Mix on medium speed until smooth and creamy, about 2-3 minutes. Reduce the speed to low and gradually add the powdered sugar. Once all the sugar is incorporated, increase the speed to medium-high and mix until fluffy. Add the vanilla extract and mix briefly to combine.
5. Assemble the Cake: Place one cake layer on a serving plate or cake stand. Spread a generous layer of frosting on top. Place the second cake layer on top and frost the top and sides of the cake with the remaining frosting. Decorate with additional chopped nuts or grated carrot, if desired.

Nutritional Value (per serving)

Calories: ~450 | Carbohydrates: 55g | Protein: 6g | Fat: 22g | Fiber: 2g | Sugar: 35g | Sodium: 350mg

Red Velvet Cake

Ingredients

For the Cake: 2½ cups (310g) all-purpose flour | 1½ cups (300g) granulated sugar | 1 teaspoon baking soda | 1 teaspoon salt | 1 teaspoon cocoa powder | 1½ cups (360ml) vegetable oil | 1 cup (240ml) buttermilk, room temperature | 2 large eggs, room temperature| 2 tablespoons red food coloring | 1 teaspoon vanilla extract | 1 teaspoon white vinegar

For the Cream Cheese Frosting: 8 oz (225g) cream cheese, softened | ½ cup (115g) unsalted butter, softened | 4 cups (500g) powdered sugar | 1 teaspoon vanilla extract

Prep Time: 20 minutes

Bake Time: 30-35 minutes.

Cooling and Frosting Time: 1 hour

Servings: One 9-inch, 2-layer cake (12 servings)

Directions

1. Preheat your oven to 350°F (175°C). Grease and flour two 9-inch round cake pans or line them with parchment paper. In a large mixing bowl, combine the flour, sugar, baking soda, salt, and cocoa powder.
2. In the bowl of your stand mixer, attach the paddle attachment. Add the vegetable oil, buttermilk, eggs, red food coloring, vanilla extract, and vinegar to the mixing bowl. Mix on medium speed until the ingredients are well combined.
3. Reduce the mixer speed to low and gradually add the dry ingredients to the wet mixture, about ½ cup at a time. Once all the dry ingredients are incorporated, increase the mixer speed to medium and beat for 1-2 minutes, ensuring a smooth and lump-free batter.

4. Divide the batter evenly between the prepared cake pans. Smooth the tops with a spatula. Bake in the preheated oven for 30-35 minutes, or until a toothpick inserted in the center comes out clean. Remove the cakes from the oven and let them cool.
5. Prepare the Cream Cheese Frosting: Clean the stand mixer bowl and attach the paddle or whisk attachment. Add the softened cream cheese and butter to the bowl. Beat on medium speed until smooth and creamy, about 2 minutes. Gradually add the powdered sugar, 1 cup at a time, mixing on low speed to prevent spillage. Once incorporated, increase the speed to medium and beat until fluffy. Add the vanilla extract and mix for another 30 seconds.
6. Assemble the Cake: Place one cake layer on a serving plate or cake stand. Spread a generous layer of cream cheese frosting on top. Add the second cake layer and frost the top and sides of the cake. Decorate as desired (e.g., with red velvet crumbs or piped frosting).

Nutritional Value (per serving)

Calories: ~450 | Carbohydrates: 55g | Protein: 5g | Fat: 22g | Fiber: 1g | Sugar: 38g | Sodium: 360mg

Lemon Pound Cake

Ingredients

For the Cake: 1 ¾ cups all-purpose flour | 1 ½ teaspoons baking powder | ½ teaspoon salt | 1 cup unsalted butter, softened | 1 ¾ cups granulated sugar | 4 large eggs | 1 teaspoon vanilla extract | 2 tablespoons fresh lemon juice | 1 tablespoon lemon zest | ½ cup whole milk

For the Glaze: 1 cup powdered sugar | 2-3 tablespoons fresh lemon juice

Prep Time: 15 minutes

Cook Time: 60-70 minutes

Servings: 8-10 slices

Directions

1. Preheat the oven to 350°F (175°C). Grease and flour a 9x5-inch loaf pan or line it with parchment paper for easy removal. In a medium bowl, whisk together the flour, baking powder, and salt. Set aside.
2. Attach the paddle attachment to your stand mixer. Add the softened butter and granulated sugar to the mixer bowl. Start on low speed, then increase to medium-high speed and cream for about 3-5 minutes, or until the mixture is light and fluffy. Scrape down the sides of the bowl as needed.
3. Reduce the speed to medium and add the eggs one at a time, beating well after each addition. This ensures the eggs are fully incorporated and the batter remains smooth. Add the vanilla extract, lemon juice, and lemon zest, and mix until combined.
4. Reduce the mixer speed to low. Add the dry ingredients in three additions, alternating with the milk in two additions, starting and ending with the dry ingredients. Mix until just combined, being careful not to overmix, as this can make the cake dense.
5. Pour the batter into the prepared loaf pan, spreading it evenly. Bake for 60-70 minutes, or until a toothpick inserted into the center comes out clean. Allow the cake to cool in the pan.
6. Prepare the Lemon Glaze: In a small bowl, whisk together the powdered sugar and lemon juice until smooth and pourable. Adjust the consistency with more lemon juice or powdered sugar as needed.
7. Once the cake is completely cool, drizzle the glaze over the top.

Nutritional Value (per serving)

Calories: ~350 | Carbohydrates: 50g | Protein: 5g | Fat: 15g | Sugar: 35g | Fiber: 1g | Sodium: 150mg

Angel Food Cake

Ingredients

For the Cake: 1 cup cake flour, sifted | 1 ½ cups granulated sugar (divided into ¾ cup and ¾ cup portions) | 1 ¼ cups egg whites (approximately 10 large eggs), at room temperature | 1 ½ teaspoons cream of tartar | ¼ teaspoon salt | 1 teaspoon vanilla extract | ½ teaspoon almond extract (optional)

Prep Time: 20 minutes

Bake Time: 35-40 minutes.

Servings: 12

Directions

1. Preheat your oven to 350°F (175°C). Ensure your stand mixer's bowl and whisk attachment are clean and dry. Any grease or moisture can prevent the egg whites from whipping properly. Sift the cake flour and ¾ cup of the granulated sugar together three times. This helps aerate the flour and ensures a delicate texture.
2. Add the room-temperature egg whites, cream of tartar, and salt to the mixer bowl. Attach the whisk attachment to your stand mixer. Start the mixer on medium-low speed, gradually increasing to medium-high speed, and whip until the mixture becomes frothy.
3. Slowly add the remaining ¾ cup of sugar, one tablespoon at a time, while continuing to whip. Add the vanilla extract and almond extract (if using) once the sugar is incorporated. Continue whipping until stiff peaks form. The egg whites should hold their shape when you lift the whisk but still appear smooth and glossy.
4. Reduce the mixer speed to low and gently fold in the sifted flour and sugar mixture in three additions. To avoid deflating the egg whites, add the dry ingredients gradually and fold using a silicone spatula or the mixer's lowest setting.
5. Pour the batter into an ungreased 10-inch tube pan. The lack of grease allows the batter to cling to the sides of the pan as it rises, ensuring the characteristic height of an Angel Food Cake. Gently run a knife through the batter to remove air pockets and smooth the top. Bake for 35-40 minutes, or until the top is golden brown and springs back when lightly touched.
6. Remove the pan from the oven and immediately invert it onto a bottle or heatproof funnel to cool. Cooling upside down prevents the cake from collapsing as it sets. Run a thin knife around the edges of the pan and the center tube to loosen the cake. Gently release it onto a serving plate.
7. Serve plain, or top with fresh berries, whipped cream, or a dusting of powdered sugar.

Nutritional Value (per serving)

Calories: ~140 | Carbohydrates: 30g | Protein: 4g | Fat: 0g | Fiber: 0g | Sugar: 22g | Sodium: 90mg

Tres Leches Cake

Ingredients

For the Cake: 1 cup all-purpose flour | 1 ½ teaspoons baking powder | ¼ teaspoon salt | 5 large eggs, separated | 1 cup granulated sugar, divided | 1 teaspoon vanilla extract | ⅓ cup whole milk

For the Milk Mixture: 1 cup evaporated milk | 1 cup sweetened condensed milk | ½ cup heavy cream

For the Whipped Topping: 1 cup heavy cream, chilled | 3 tablespoons powdered sugar | 1 teaspoon vanilla extract

Prep Time: 20 minutes

Cook Time: 25 minutes.

Soaking Time: 2 hours (or overnight)

Servings: 12

Directions

1. Preheat the oven to 350°F (175°C) and grease a 9x13-inch baking dish. In a medium bowl, sift together the flour, baking powder, and salt. Set aside.
2. Using your stand mixer with the whisk attachment, beat the egg whites on medium-high speed until soft peaks form (about 3-4 minutes). Gradually add ½ cup of granulated sugar while continuing to whisk until stiff peaks form. Transfer to a clean bowl and set aside.
3. In the same mixing bowl (no need to wash), combine the egg yolks and the remaining ½ cup of granulated sugar. Whisk on medium speed until the mixture is pale and thick (about 3 minutes). Add vanilla extract and whole milk, and whisk briefly to combine.

4. Switch to the paddle attachment. Add the dry ingredients to the yolk mixture in batches, mixing on low speed until just combined. Gently fold the whipped egg whites into the batter using a spatula, maintaining as much air as possible.
5. Pour the batter into the prepared baking dish, smoothing the surface with a spatula. Bake for 20-25 minutes, or until a toothpick inserted into the center comes out clean.
6. Prepare the Milk Mixture: In a medium bowl, whisk together the evaporated milk, condensed milk, and heavy cream until smooth.
7. Once the cake has cooled, use a fork or skewer to poke holes all over the surface. Slowly pour the milk mixture over the cake, allowing it to soak in gradually. Cover the dish with plastic wrap and refrigerate for at least 2 hours or overnight for maximum flavor absorption.
8. Make the Whipped Topping: Clean the mixer bowl and attach the whisk attachment. Add the chilled heavy cream, powdered sugar, and vanilla extract. Whip on high speed until stiff peaks form (about 2-3 minutes). Be careful not to overwhip.
9. Spread the whipped topping evenly over the soaked cake.

Nutritional Value (per serving)

Calories: ~350 | Carbohydrates: 45g | Protein: 6g | Fat: 15g | Sugar: 30g | Fiber: 0g | Sodium: 140mg

Hummingbird Cake

Ingredients

For the Cake: 3 cups all-purpose flour | 2 cups granulated sugar | 1 teaspoon baking soda | 1 teaspoon ground cinnamon | ½ teaspoon ground nutmeg | ½ teaspoon salt | 3 large eggs, room temperature | 1 ¼ cups vegetable oil | 1 ½ teaspoons vanilla extract | 1 cup mashed ripe bananas (about 2 large bananas) | 1 (8-ounce) can crushed pineapple, undrained | 1 cup chopped pecans or walnuts (optional)

For the Cream Cheese Frosting: 16 ounces cream cheese, softened | 1 cup unsalted butter, softened | 4 cups powdered sugar, sifted | 2 teaspoons vanilla extract

Prep Time: 20 minutes

Baking Time: 25–30 minutes

Servings: Makes 12

Directions

1. Preheat your oven to 350°F (175°C).Grease and flour three 9-inch round cake pans or line them with parchment paper.
2. Mix the Dry Ingredients: Attach the flat beater to your stand mixer. In the mixing bowl, combine the flour, sugar, baking soda, cinnamon, nutmeg, and salt. Mix on low speed until evenly combined.
3. In a separate bowl, whisk together the eggs, vegetable oil, and vanilla extract. Gradually add the mixture to the dry ingredients in the stand mixer on low speed, mixing just until combined.
4. Stir in the mashed bananas and crushed pineapple (with juice) using the stand mixer on medium-low speed. If using nuts, fold them in gently with a spatula or the stand mixer on its lowest speed. Avoid overmixing.
5. Divide the batter evenly among the prepared pans. Bake for 25–30 minutes, or until a toothpick inserted in the center comes out clean. Allow the cakes to cool in the pans.
6. Prepare the Cream Cheese Frosting: Clean the mixing bowl and attach the paddle attachment. Beat the cream cheese and butter on medium speed until smooth and creamy, about 2–3 minutes. Gradually add the powdered sugar, 1 cup at a time, mixing on low speed to avoid splattering. Increase to medium speed and beat until fluffy. Add the vanilla extract and mix until incorporated.
7. Place one cake layer on a serving plate or cake stand. Spread a generous layer of cream cheese frosting on top. Add the second cake layer and repeat. Top with the final layer and frost the top and sides.

Nutritional Value (per serving)

Calories: ~650 | Carbohydrates: 80g | Protein: 6g | Fat: 35g | Fiber: 2g | Sugar: 55g | Sodium: 300mg

Coconut Layer Cake

Ingredients

For the Cake: 2 ½ cups all-purpose flour | 2 ½ teaspoons baking powder | ½ teaspoon baking soda | ½ teaspoon salt | 1 cup unsalted butter, softened | 2 cups granulated sugar | 4 large eggs, room temperature | 1 cup coconut milk (full-fat for richer flavor) | 1 teaspoon vanilla extract | 1 cup unsweetened shredded coconut | ½ teaspoon coconut extract (optional, for extra coconut flavor)

For the Frosting: 1 cup unsalted butter, softened | 8 oz cream cheese, softened | 4 cups powdered sugar, sifted | 2 teaspoons vanilla extract | ½ teaspoon coconut extract (optional) | 1 ½ cups unsweetened shredded coconut (for garnish)

Prep Time: 20 minutes

Cook Time: 25-30 minutes

Servings: 10-12

Directions

1. Preheat your oven to 350°F (175°C). Grease and flour two 9-inch round cake pans or line them with parchment paper.
2. In the bowl of your stand mixer, combine the flour, baking powder, baking soda, and salt. Use the flat beater attachment on low speed to mix the dry ingredients together until well combined.
3. In a separate bowl, cream together the softened butter and sugar using the stand mixer with the flat beater attachment on medium speed until light and fluffy. This should take about 4-5 minutes.
4. Add the eggs one at a time, beating well after each addition. Scrape down the sides of the bowl as needed. Gradually add the coconut milk, vanilla extract, and coconut extract (if using) to the butter and sugar mixture, beating on low speed until combined.

5. Slowly add the dry ingredients to the wet mixture, alternating with the shredded coconut, starting and ending with the dry ingredients. Mix just until combined, ensuring not to overmix. Divide the batter evenly between the two prepared cake pans and smooth the tops with a spatula.
6. Bake in the preheated oven for 25-30 minutes or until a toothpick inserted into the center of the cakes comes out clean. Let the cakes cool in the pans.
7. Prepare the Frosting: In the bowl of your stand mixer, combine the softened butter and cream cheese. Use the flat beater attachment to mix on medium speed until smooth and creamy, about 3-4 minutes.
8. Gradually add the sifted powdered sugar, a cup at a time, mixing on low speed until incorporated. Once all the sugar is added, increase the speed to medium-high and beat until the frosting is light and fluffy, about 3-5 minutes. Add the vanilla extract and coconut extract (if using) and mix until combined.
9. Assemble the Cake: Once the cakes are completely cooled, place the first cake layer on a serving platter. Spread a layer of frosting over the top. Place the second cake layer on top and frost the entire cake with the cream cheese frosting. Press the shredded coconut into the sides and top of the cake for decoration.
10. If you prefer, refrigerate the cake for about 30 minutes to set the frosting before serving. This helps the cake and frosting hold together better when slicing.

Nutritional Value (per serving)

Calories: ~450 | Carbohydrates: 58g | Protein: 5g | Fat: 25g | Fiber: 2g | Sugar: 38g | Sodium: 210mg

Tip: To toast coconut flakes: Place unsweetened shredded coconut on a baking sheet and toast at 350°F (175°C) for 5-10 minutes, stirring occasionally, until golden brown. This adds extra flavor and crunch to your cake.

Funfetti Cake

Ingredients

For the Cake: 2 ¾ cups all-purpose flour | 2 ½ teaspoons baking powder | ½ teaspoon salt | 1 cup unsalted butter, softened | 1 ¾ cups granulated sugar | 4 large eggs | 2 teaspoons pure vanilla extract | 1 cup whole milk | ¾ cup rainbow sprinkles

For the Frosting: 1 cup unsalted butter, softened | 4 cups powdered sugar, sifted | 2 teaspoons pure vanilla extract | 2-3 tablespoons heavy cream (adjust for desired consistency) | Extra sprinkles for decoration

Prep Time: 20 minutes

Bake Time: 30-35 minutes

Servings: One 9-inch, 2-layer cake (serves 12-16)

Directions

1. In a medium bowl, whisk together the flour, baking powder, and salt. Set aside.
2. Attach the flat beater to your stand mixer. Place the softened butter and sugar into the mixer bowl. Mix on medium speed for 2-3 minutes, or until the mixture is light, fluffy, and pale in color. This step creates air pockets for a tender cake.
3. With the mixer on low speed, add the eggs one at a time, mixing well after each addition to ensure full incorporation. Add the vanilla extract and mix briefly to combine.
4. Reduce the mixer speed to low. Add one-third of the dry ingredients, followed by half of the milk. Repeat, ending with the last third of the dry ingredients. Mix just until combined, scraping down the sides of the bowl as needed.

5. Detach the bowl from the stand mixer. Gently fold in the rainbow sprinkles using a spatula to evenly distribute them throughout the batter without overmixing. This prevents the sprinkles from bleeding too much color.
6. Preheat the oven to 350°F (175°C). Grease and flour two 9-inch round cake pans or line them with parchment paper. Divide the batter evenly between the pans and smooth the tops with a spatula. Bake for 30-35 minutes, or until a toothpick inserted into the center comes out clean. Cool the cakes in the pans for 10 minutes.
7. Make the Frosting: Clean the stand mixer bowl and attach the flat beater or whisk attachment. Beat the butter on medium speed until creamy. Gradually add the powdered sugar, one cup at a time, mixing on low speed until incorporated. Add the vanilla extract and 2 tablespoons of heavy cream. Increase the speed to medium-high and beat until the frosting is smooth and fluffy.
8. Place one cake layer on a serving plate. Spread a generous layer of frosting over the top. Add the second cake layer and frost the top and sides.

Nutritional Value (per serving)

Calories: ~450 | Carbohydrates: 58g | Protein: 5g | Fat: 22g | Fiber: 1g | Sugar: 40g | Sodium: 150mg

Tip: Lightly toss the sprinkles in a small amount of flour before folding them into the batter. This keeps them evenly distributed throughout the cake.

Black Forest Cake

Ingredients

For the Cake: 1 ¾ cups all-purpose flour | ¾ cup unsweetened cocoa powder | 1 ½ teaspoons baking powder | ½ teaspoon baking soda | ½ teaspoon salt | 1 ¾ cups granulated sugar | ¾ cup unsalted butter, softened | 3 large eggs | 1 teaspoon vanilla extract | 1 cup buttermilk

For the Filling: 1 cup cherry preserves or canned cherry pie filling | ½ cup kirsch (cherry brandy), optional

For the Whipped Cream: 2 cups heavy whipping cream, chilled | ½ cup powdered sugar | 1 teaspoon vanilla extract

For Decoration: 1 cup dark chocolate shavings| Fresh cherries (optional)

Prep Time: 30 minutes

Baking Time: 30 minutes

Servings: 8-10 slices

Directions

1. Preheat your oven to 350°F (175°C). Grease and line two 8-inch round cake pans with parchment paper. In the bowl of your stand mixer, sift together the flour, cocoa powder, baking powder, baking soda, and salt.
2. Attach the flat beater attachment and mix the dry ingredients on low speed to combine. Add the sugar and butter to the bowl. Mix on medium speed until light and fluffy, about 3-4 minutes. Scrape down the sides of the bowl as needed.
3. With the mixer on low, add the eggs one at a time, followed by the vanilla extract. Increase speed to medium and beat until smooth. Reduce speed to low and alternate adding the buttermilk and dry ingredients in three additions, beginning and ending with the dry ingredients. Mix until just combined—do not overmix.
4. Divide the batter evenly between the prepared pans and smooth the tops with a spatula. Bake in the preheated oven for 25-30 minutes, or until a toothpick inserted into the center comes out clean. Let the cakes cool in the pans.
5. Prepare the Whipped Cream: Once the cakes have cooled, clean the mixer bowl and attach the whisk attachment. Pour the chilled heavy whipping cream into the bowl. Add the powdered sugar and vanilla extract. Whip on medium-high speed until stiff peaks form, about 3-4 minutes.
6. Place one cake layer on a serving plate or cake stand. Brush the top of the cake with kirsch (optional) and spread a layer of cherry preserves evenly over the surface. Spread a generous layer of whipped cream over the cherries. Place the second cake layer on top and repeat the process.
7. Decorate the Cake: Press chocolate shavings onto the sides of the cake. Sprinkle additional shavings on top. Chill the assembled cake for at least 30 minutes before slicing.

Nutritional Value (per slice)

Calories: ~450 | Carbohydrates: 52g | Protein: 6g | Fat: 25g | Fiber: 3g | Sugar: 35g | Sodium: 180mg

Tip: To make the whipped cream last longer, add 1 teaspoon of gelatin dissolved in 2 tablespoons of water while whipping.

Cheesecake

Ingredients

For the Crust: 1 ½ cups graham cracker crumbs | ¼ cup granulated sugar | ½ cup unsalted butter, melted

For the Filling: 4 (8 oz) packages cream cheese, softened | 1 cup granulated sugar | 1 teaspoon vanilla extract | 4 large eggs | 1 cup sour cream | 2 tablespoons all-purpose flour

For the Topping (optional): Fresh fruit, fruit compote, or whipped cream

Prep Time: 20 minutes

Bake Time: 50-60 minutes

Servings: 8-10 slices

Directions

1. Preheat your oven to 325°F (160°C). In a medium mixing bowl, combine the graham cracker crumbs, sugar, and melted butter. Stir until the mixture resembles wet sand.
2. Press the mixture into the bottom of a 9-inch springform pan to form an even layer. Bake the crust for 8-10 minutes, then set aside to cool.
3. Prepare the Cheesecake Filling: Attach the paddle attachment to your stand mixer. In the stand mixer bowl, beat the softened cream cheese on medium speed until smooth and creamy, about 2-3 minutes. Scrape down the sides of the bowl to ensure even mixing.

4. Gradually add the sugar and continue mixing until fully incorporated and smooth. Add the vanilla extract and mix for 30 seconds. Reduce the mixer speed to low and add the eggs one at a time, beating well after each addition.
5. Avoid overmixing to prevent air bubbles, which can cause cracks in the cheesecake. Add the sour cream and flour, mixing just until combined. Scrape the sides and bottom of the bowl to ensure a uniform batter.
6. Pour the cheesecake filling over the prepared crust, spreading it evenly with a spatula. Place the springform pan on a baking sheet. To prevent cracks, you can bake the cheesecake in a water bath by placing the pan in a larger dish and pouring boiling water around it (optional but recommended). Bake at 325°F (160°C) for 50-60 minutes, or until the edges are set and the center jiggles slightly when gently shaken.
7. Remove the cheesecake from the oven and let it cool to room temperature. Cover the cheesecake and refrigerate for at least 3 hours or overnight to set.

Nutritional Value (per slice)

Calories: ~350 | Carbohydrates: 30g | Protein: 6g | Fat: 25g | Fiber: 1g | Sugar: 20g | Sodium: 250mg

PIE AND TART

41. Classic Pie Crust

42. Apple Pie

43. Lemon Meringue Tart

44. Chocolate Ganache Tart

45. Quiche Lorraine

46. Mini Fruit Tarts

47. Blueberry Crumble Tart

48. Pumpkin Pie

49. Pecan Pie

50. Pear and Almond Tart (Tarte Bourdaloue)

51. Coconut Cream Pie

52. French Silk Pie

53. Cheese and Spinach Tart

Classic Pie Crust

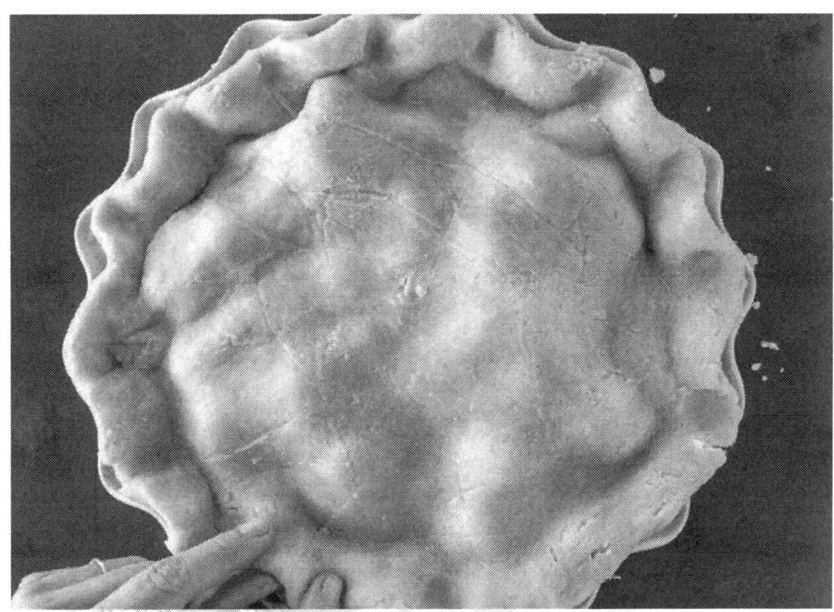

Ingredients

2 ½ cups all-purpose flour | 1 teaspoon salt | 1 tablespoon granulated sugar (optional, for sweet crusts) | 1 cup unsalted butter, cold and cut into small cubes | 6-8 tablespoons ice water

Prep Time: 15 minutes

Chill Time: 1 hour

Servings: Two 9-inch pie crusts

Directions

1. Ensure the butter is cold and cubed before starting. Place it in the refrigerator to keep it firm. Fill a small bowl with ice water and set aside.
2. Attach the flat beater to your stand mixer. In the mixer bowl, combine the flour, salt, and sugar (if using). Mix on low speed for 10-15 seconds to combine.
3. Add the cold, cubed butter to the flour mixture. Mix on low speed until the mixture resembles coarse crumbs with pea-sized pieces of butter. This should take about 1-2 minutes. With the mixer on low speed, add 1 tablespoon of ice water at a time. Continue adding water until the dough begins to come together but is not sticky. You may not need all the water.
4. Transfer the dough onto a lightly floured surface. Divide it into two equal portions. Shape each portion into a flat disc, wrap tightly in plastic wrap, and refrigerate for at least 1 hour (or up to 2 days).
5. On a floured surface, roll out one disc of dough to fit a 9-inch pie pan. Use a rolling pin and work from the center outward, turning the dough occasionally to maintain an even thickness.

6. Transfer the rolled-out dough to the pie pan, pressing gently to fit. Trim excess dough, leaving about 1 inch overhang for crimping. Repeat with the second disc if making a double-crust pie or save it for another use.
7. For a pre-baked crust: Prick the bottom with a fork, line with parchment paper, and fill with pie weights. Bake at 375°F (190°C) for 15 minutes, then remove weights and bake another 5-7 minutes until lightly golden.
8. For a filled pie: Add your filling and bake according to the specific pie recipe.

Nutritional Value (per serving)

Calories: ~200 | Carbohydrates: 17g | Protein: 2g | Fat: 14g | Fiber: 1g | Sugar: 1g (varies by sugar addition) | Sodium: 90mg

Apple Pie

Ingredients

For the Crust: 2 ½ cups all-purpose flour | 1 teaspoon salt| 1 teaspoon granulated sugar | 1 cup (2 sticks) unsalted butter, chilled and cubed | 6-8 tablespoons ice water

For the Filling: 6 cups peeled, cored, and sliced apples (Granny Smith or Honeycrisp) | ¾ cup granulated sugar | ¼ cup brown sugar | 1 tablespoon lemon juice | 2 tablespoons all-purpose flour | 1 teaspoon cinnamon| ¼ teaspoon nutmeg | ¼ teaspoon salt

For the Egg Wash: 1 large egg, beaten | 1 tablespoon milk

Prep Time: 30 minutes

Bake Time: 50-60 minutes

Servings: 8 slices

Directions

1. Attach the paddle attachment to your stand mixer. Add the flour, salt, and sugar to the mixer bowl. Mix on low speed for 10-15 seconds to combine. Add the chilled butter cubes and mix on medium-low speed until the mixture resembles coarse crumbs with some pea-sized pieces of butter. This should take about 1-2 minutes.
2. Gradually add the ice water, 1 tablespoon at a time, while mixing on low speed until the dough starts to come together. Avoid overmixing; the dough should still have visible bits of butter. Divide the dough into two equal portions, shape into disks, wrap in plastic wrap, and refrigerate for at least 30 minutes.
3. Prepare the Filling: In a large mixing bowl, combine the apple slices, granulated sugar, brown sugar, lemon juice, flour, cinnamon, nutmeg, and salt. Use your stand mixer with the flat beater attachment to gently mix the filling on low speed for 1-2 minutes. This ensures the apples are evenly coated with the spices and sugar.
4. Preheat your oven to 375°F (190°C). Roll out one disk of dough on a lightly floured surface to fit a 9-inch pie pan. Place the rolled dough into the pan and trim any excess, leaving about 1 inch of overhang.
5. Fill the crust with the prepared apple filling, spreading it evenly. Roll out the second disk of dough to create the top crust. You can either cover the pie completely or cut strips to form a lattice pattern. Seal the edges by crimping with your fingers or a fork. If using a full crust, cut slits in the top to allow steam to escape.
6. Brush the top crust with the egg wash (beaten egg mixed with milk) for a golden finish. Place the pie on a baking sheet to catch any drips and bake for 50-60 minutes, or until the crust is golden brown and the filling is bubbling. If the edges brown too quickly, cover them with aluminum foil midway through baking.
7. Serve warm or at room temperature.

Nutritional Value (per slice)

Calories: ~350 | Carbohydrates: 50g | Protein: 4g | Fat: 15g | Fiber: 3g | Sugar: 25g | Sodium: 200mg

Lemon Meringue Tart

Ingredients

For the Tart Crust: 1 ¾ cups (220g) all-purpose flour | ½ cup (113g) unsalted butter, chilled and cubed | ¼ cup (50g) granulated sugar | 1 large egg yolk | 2–3 tablespoons ice water

For the Lemon Filling: 1 cup (200g) granulated sugar | ⅓ cup (43g) cornstarch | 1 cup (240ml) water | ½ cup (120ml) fresh lemon juice| 1 tablespoon lemon zest | 3 large egg yolks | 2 tablespoons unsalted butter

For the Meringue: 3 large egg whites | ½ cup (100g) granulated sugar | ¼ teaspoon cream of tartar | 1 teaspoon vanilla extract

Prep Time: 30 minutes

Bake Time: 20-25 minutes

Servings: 6–8

Directions

1. Attach the paddle attachment to your stand mixer. In the stand mixer bowl, combine the flour and sugar on low speed for 30 seconds. Add the chilled, cubed butter and mix on medium speed until the mixture resembles coarse crumbs.
2. Add the egg yolk and mix briefly. Gradually add the ice water, 1 tablespoon at a time, mixing just until the dough starts to come together. Avoid overmixing. Remove the dough from the bowl, shape it into a disk, wrap it in plastic wrap, and refrigerate for 30 minutes.
3. Preheat the oven to 375°F (190°C). Roll out the chilled dough on a lightly floured surface and transfer it to a tart pan. Press the dough into the edges and trim any excess.

4. Prick the base with a fork, line with parchment paper, and fill with pie weights or dried beans. Bake for 15 minutes, then remove the weights and bake for another 5–7 minutes until golden. Let it cool.
5. Make the Lemon Filling: In a medium saucepan, whisk together sugar and cornstarch. Gradually add water, lemon juice, and zest, stirring until smooth. Cook over medium heat, stirring constantly, until the mixture thickens and starts to bubble.
6. Reduce the heat to low and whisk in the egg yolks, one at a time. Continue stirring for 2 minutes, then remove from heat. Add butter and stir until fully melted and incorporated. Let the filling cool slightly before pouring into the baked tart shell.
7. Attach the whisk attachment to your stand mixer. Add the egg whites and cream of tartar to the mixer bowl. Beat on medium speed until soft peaks form. Gradually add sugar, 1 tablespoon at a time, and continue beating on high speed until stiff, glossy peaks form (about 5–7 minutes). Mix in the vanilla extract.
8. Spoon or pipe the meringue onto the lemon filling, spreading it to cover the edges completely to seal.
9. Bake the tart at 375°F (190°C) for 8–10 minutes, or until the meringue is golden brown. Let the tart cool to room temperature, then refrigerate for at least 1 hour before serving.

Nutritional Value (per serving)

Calories: ~320 | Carbohydrates: 45g | Protein: 5g | Fat: 12g | Fiber: 1g | Sugar: 30g | Sodium: 120mg

Tips: For best results, chill the stand mixer bowl and whisk attachment for 15 minutes before whipping the egg whites.

Chocolate Ganache Tart

Ingredients

For the Tart Crust: 1 ¼ cups all-purpose flour | ½ cup unsalted butter, cold and cubed | ¼ cup granulated sugar | 1 large egg yolk | 1-2 tablespoons cold water

For the Ganache Filling: 1 cup heavy cream | 8 ounces semi-sweet or dark chocolate, finely chopped | 2 tablespoons unsalted butter, softened | 1 teaspoon vanilla extract

For Garnish (optional): Fresh berries | Shaved chocolate | Sea salt flakes

Prep Time: 25 minutes

Bake Time: 15-20 minutes

Servings: 8 slices

Directions

1. Attach the paddle attachment to your stand mixer. In the mixer bowl, combine the flour, sugar, and a pinch of salt. Mix on low speed for a few seconds to combine.
2. Add the cold, cubed butter to the bowl and mix on low to medium speed until the mixture resembles coarse crumbs. Add the egg yolk and mix briefly. Gradually add cold water, 1 tablespoon at a time, until the dough begins to come together. Avoid overmixing to keep the crust tender. Form the dough into a disk, wrap it in plastic wrap, and refrigerate for at least 30 minutes.
3. Preheat your oven to 350°F (175°C). Roll out the chilled dough on a lightly floured surface to fit a 9-inch tart pan. Press the dough evenly into the pan and trim any excess. Prick the bottom with a fork to prevent puffing.
4. Line the tart shell with parchment paper and fill it with pie weights or dried beans. Bake for 15-20 minutes, or until the edges are golden. Remove the weights and parchment paper, then bake for another 5 minutes. Let the crust cool completely.
5. Prepare the Ganache Filling: Heat the heavy cream in a small saucepan over medium heat until it just begins to simmer (do not boil).
6. Attach the whisk attachment to your stand mixer. Place the chopped chocolate in the mixer bowl. Pour the hot cream over the chocolate and let it sit for 2-3 minutes to melt. Whisk on low speed until the mixture is smooth and glossy. Add the butter and vanilla extract, and whisk on low speed until fully incorporated.
7. Pour the ganache into the cooled tart shell, spreading it evenly with a spatula. Tap the tart gently on the counter to remove any air bubbles. Refrigerate the tart for 2-3 hours, or until the ganache is set.

Nutritional Value (per slice)

Calories: ~350 | Carbohydrates: 25g | Protein: 4g | Fat: 25g | Fiber: 2g | Sugar: 15g | Sodium: 50mg

Quiche Lorraine

Ingredients

For the Crust: 1 ½ cups all-purpose flour | ½ teaspoon salt | ½ cup (1 stick) unsalted butter, cold and cubed | 3-4 tablespoons ice water

For the Filling: 6 slices bacon, cooked and crumbled | 1 cup Gruyère cheese, shredded (or Swiss cheese) | 3 large eggs | 1 cup heavy cream | ½ cup whole milk | ½ teaspoon salt | ¼ teaspoon ground nutmeg | ¼ teaspoon black pepper

Prep Time: 30 minutes

Cook Time: 35-40 minutes

Servings: 6-8 slices

Directions

1. Attach the paddle attachment to your stand mixer. In the mixer bowl, combine the flour and salt on low speed for 10 seconds. Add the cold, cubed butter and mix on medium-low speed until the mixture resembles coarse crumbs, with pea-sized pieces of butter.
2. Gradually add the ice water, 1 tablespoon at a time, mixing on low speed until the dough comes together. Be careful not to overmix. Shape the dough into a disk, wrap it in plastic wrap, and refrigerate for at least 30 minutes.
3. Preheat your oven to 375°F (190°C). Roll out the chilled dough on a lightly floured surface to fit a 9-inch tart pan or pie dish. Press the dough into the pan, trimming any excess from the edges. Prick the base with a fork to prevent puffing during baking.
4. Line the crust with parchment paper and fill it with pie weights or dried beans. Bake the crust for 10-12 minutes, then remove the weights and parchment paper and bake for another 5 minutes until lightly golden.

5. Prepare the Filling: Clean and dry the mixer bowl, then attach the whisk attachment. In the mixer bowl, whisk the eggs on medium speed until slightly frothy, about 1 minute. Add the heavy cream, milk, salt, nutmeg, and pepper, and whisk on low speed until well combined. Stir in the crumbled bacon and shredded cheese using a spatula.
6. Pour the filling into the prebaked crust, spreading it evenly. Place the tart pan on a baking sheet to catch any spills. Bake at 375°F (190°C) for 35-40 minutes, or until the custard is set and the top is golden brown. The center should jiggle slightly when gently shaken.

Nutritional Value (per slice)

Calories: ~350 | Carbohydrates: 15g | Protein: 12g | Fat: 25g | Fiber: 1g | Sugar: 2g | Sodium: 500mg

Mini Fruit Tarts

Ingredients

For the Tart Shells: 1 ½ cups all-purpose flour | ½ cup unsalted butter, chilled and cubed | ¼ cup powdered sugar | 1 large egg yolk | 2 tablespoons cold water

For the Custard Filling: 1 ½ cups whole milk | ½ cup granulated sugar | 3 large egg yolks | 2 tablespoons cornstarch | 1 teaspoon vanilla extract | 2 tablespoons unsalted butter

For the Topping: Assorted fresh fruits (berries, kiwi, mango, etc.) | 2 tablespoons apricot jam, warmed (for glaze)

Prep Time: 30 minutes

Chilling Time: 30 minutes

Bake Time: 20 minutes

Servings: 12 mini tarts

Directions

1. Attach the paddle attachment to your stand mixer. In the mixer bowl, combine the flour and powdered sugar on low speed. Add the chilled butter cubes and mix until the mixture resembles coarse crumbs.
2. Add the egg yolk and cold water, mixing just until the dough starts to come together. Be careful not to overmix. Remove the dough from the mixer, shape it into a disk, wrap it in plastic wrap, and refrigerate for 30 minutes.
3. Preheat your oven to 350°F (175°C). Roll out the chilled dough on a lightly floured surface to about ⅛-inch thickness.
4. Cut circles slightly larger than your tartlet molds and press them into the molds, trimming the excess dough. Prick the bottom of each shell with a fork and bake for 15-20 minutes, or until golden brown. Let it cool completely before filling.
5. Prepare the Custard Filling: Attach the whisk attachment to your stand mixer. In a medium saucepan, heat the milk until steaming but not boiling. In the mixer bowl, whisk together the sugar, egg yolks, and cornstarch on medium speed until pale and thick, about 2 minutes.
6. Slowly add the hot milk to the egg mixture, whisking constantly to prevent curdling. Transfer the mixture back to the saucepan and cook over medium heat, whisking continuously, until thickened and bubbling. Remove from heat, stir in the vanilla extract and butter, and let cool slightly.
7. Spoon or pipe the custard filling into the cooled tart shells. Arrange the fresh fruits on top, brush the fruits with the warmed apricot jam.

Nutritional Value (per tart)

Calories: ~180 | Carbohydrates: 25g | Protein: 3g | Fat: 8g | Fiber: 1g | Sugar: 12g | Sodium: 40mg

Blueberry Crumble Tart

Ingredients

For the Tart Crust: 1 ½ cups all-purpose flour | ½ cup powdered sugar | ½ teaspoon salt | ½ cup unsalted butter, cold and cubed | 1 large egg yolk | 2-3 tablespoons cold water

For the Blueberry Filling: 3 cups fresh or frozen blueberries| ½ cup granulated sugar | 2 tablespoons cornstarch | 1 tablespoon lemon juice | 1 teaspoon lemon zest

For the Crumble Topping: ¾ cup all-purpose flour | ½ cup rolled oats | ⅓ cup brown sugar | ½ teaspoon ground cinnamon | ¼ cup unsalted butter, melted

Prep Time: 30 minutes

Bake Time: 40-50 minutes

Servings: 8-10 slices

Directions

1. Attach the paddle attachment to your stand mixer. In the mixing bowl, combine the flour, powdered sugar, and salt. Mix on low speed for 30 seconds. Add the cold, cubed butter and mix on medium speed until the mixture resembles coarse crumbs, about 2-3 minutes.
2. Add the egg yolk and 2 tablespoons of cold water. Mix on low speed just until the dough comes together. Add another tablespoon of water if necessary. Form the dough into a disk, wrap it in plastic wrap, and refrigerate for 20-30 minutes.
3. Prepare the Blueberry Filling: In a medium bowl, combine the blueberries, sugar, cornstarch, lemon juice, and zest. Toss to coat evenly. Set aside.

4. Prepare the Crumble Topping: Clean the mixing bowl and switch to the paddle attachment. Add the flour, oats, brown sugar, and cinnamon to the bowl. Mix on low speed to combine. Gradually pour in the melted butter while the mixer runs on low speed until the mixture forms large crumbs. Set aside.
5. Preheat the oven to 375°F (190°C). Roll out the chilled tart dough on a lightly floured surface to fit a 9-inch tart pan with a removable bottom. Press the dough evenly into the pan and trim any excess.
6. Spread the prepared blueberry filling evenly over the tart crust. Sprinkle the crumble topping over the blueberries, covering the filling evenly.
7. Place the tart on a baking sheet to catch any drips. Bake at 375°F (190°C) for 40-50 minutes, or until the crust is golden brown, the topping is crisp, and the blueberry filling is bubbling.

Nutritional Value (per slice)

Calories: ~320 | Carbohydrates: 45g | Protein: 4g | Fat: 14g | Fiber: 3g | Sugar: 22g | Sodium: 90mg

Pumpkin Pie

Ingredients

For the Pie Crust: 1 ½ cups all-purpose flour | ¼ teaspoon salt | ½ cup unsalted butter, cold and cut into cubes | 2-4 tablespoons ice water

For the Pumpkin Filling: 2 cups pumpkin puree (fresh or canned) | ¾ cup granulated sugar | ½ cup packed brown sugar | 1 ½ teaspoons ground cinnamon | ½ teaspoon ground ginger | ¼ teaspoon ground cloves | ½ teaspoon salt | 3 large eggs | 1 ½ cups heavy cream | 1 teaspoon vanilla extract

Prep Time: 15 minutes

Cook Time: 50-60 minutes

Servings: 8 slices

Directions

1. In the bowl of your stand mixer, attach the flat beater attachment. Add the flour and salt, and mix on low speed to combine. Gradually add the cold butter cubes and mix on low speed until the mixture resembles coarse crumbs, with pea-sized pieces of butter still visible.
2. With the mixer running on low, slowly add ice water, 1 tablespoon at a time, until the dough just begins to come together. Turn the dough out onto a lightly floured surface and knead gently into a ball. Flatten the dough into a disk, wrap in plastic wrap, and refrigerate for at least 30 minutes before rolling out.
3. Prepare the Pumpkin Filling: After refrigerating the dough, preheat your oven to 375°F (190°C). While the crust is chilling, place the pumpkin puree, sugars, cinnamon, ginger, cloves, and salt into the stand mixer bowl. Attach the paddle attachment and mix on low speed until fully combined.
4. Add the eggs, one at a time, mixing on low speed after each addition. Add the heavy cream and vanilla extract and mix on low until smooth and well incorporated. Scrape down the sides of the bowl as needed.
5. Roll out the chilled pie dough on a floured surface into a 12-inch circle. Carefully transfer the dough into a 9-inch pie pan, gently pressing it into the bottom and up the sides. Trim any excess dough and crimp the edges. Pour the prepared pumpkin filling into the pie crust, smoothing the top with a spatula.
6. Place the pie on the center rack of the oven and bake at 375°F (190°C) for 50-60 minutes. The pie is done when the filling is set around the edges but slightly jiggly in the center. If the crust begins to brown too quickly, cover the edges with aluminum foil or a pie shield to prevent burning.

Nutritional Value (per slice)

Calories: ~320 | Carbohydrates: 45g | Protein: 4g | Fat: 14g | Fiber: 3g | Sugar: 25g | Sodium: 200mg

Tips: Chill the dough for at least 30 minutes before rolling out. This ensures the butter stays cold, leading to a flakier crust.

Pecan Pie

Ingredients

For the Pie Crust: 1 ¼ cups all-purpose flour | 1 tablespoon granulated sugar | ½ teaspoon salt | 8 tablespoons (1 stick) unsalted butter, cold and cut into cubes | 3-4 tablespoons ice water

For the Filling: 1 cup light corn syrup| 1 cup packed brown sugar | 1 tablespoon unsalted butter, melted | 1 teaspoon vanilla extract | 3 large eggs | 2 cups pecan halves (toasted if preferred)

Prep Time: 20 minutes

Chilling Time: 30 minutes

Bake Time: 50-60 minutes

Servings: 8 slices

Directions

1. Attach the flat beater attachment to your stand mixer. In the mixer bowl, combine the flour, sugar, and salt. Add the cold butter cubes to the flour mixture. Mix on low speed for about 30 seconds until the mixture resembles coarse crumbs, with pea-sized pieces of butter.
2. Slowly add the ice water, 1 tablespoon at a time, and mix until the dough starts to come together. Avoid overmixing. You may need to add more water if the dough is too dry. Turn the dough out onto a floured surface, press it into a disk, and wrap it in plastic wrap. Refrigerate the dough for at least 30 minutes to firm up.
3. Prepare the Pie Filling: In the clean stand mixer bowl, attach the whisk attachment. Add the corn syrup, brown sugar, melted butter, and vanilla extract to the bowl. Mix on medium speed until smooth and combined.

4. Add the eggs, one at a time, mixing well after each addition. Continue mixing until the filling is smooth and slightly thickened. Stir in the pecans and set the mixture aside.
5. Preheat your oven to 350°F (175°C). On a floured surface, roll the chilled dough into a circle large enough to fit into a 9-inch pie pan. Transfer the rolled dough to the pie pan and trim any excess dough, leaving about 1 inch around the edges. Fold the edges over and crimp with a fork or your fingers to form a decorative border.
6. Pour the pecan pie filling into the prepared pie crust, spreading the pecans evenly. Bake the pie at 350°F (175°C) for 50-60 minutes, or until the filling is set and slightly puffed, and the crust is golden brown. If the crust edges are browning too quickly, cover them with foil to prevent burning.

Nutritional Value (per slice)

Calories: ~400 | Carbohydrates: 50g | Protein: 4g | Fat: 22g | Fiber: 3g | Sugar: 30g | Sodium: 150mg

Tips: Toasting the pecans enhances their flavor and adds a rich depth to the filling.

Pear and Almond Tart (Tarte Bourdaloue)

Ingredients

For the Tart Crust: 1 ¼ cups all-purpose flour | 2 tablespoons granulated sugar | ¼ teaspoon salt | 8 tablespoons cold unsalted butter, cubed | 1 large egg yolk | 2-3 tablespoons ice water

For the Almond Cream (Frangipane): ½ cup unsalted butter, softened | ½ cup granulated sugar | 1 large egg | 1 teaspoon vanilla extract | 1 cup almond meal (ground almonds) | 1 tablespoon all-purpose flour | 2 tablespoons heavy cream | 1 pinch salt

For the Topping: 2 ripe pears, peeled, cored, and sliced | Powdered sugar, for dusting (optional)

Prep Time: 30 minutes

Cook Time: 45-50 minutes

Servings: 8-10 slices

Directions

1. In the bowl of your stand mixer, attach the flat beater attachment. Add the flour, sugar, and salt to the bowl. Mix on low speed to combine. Add the cold, cubed butter and mix on low speed until the mixture resembles coarse crumbs. This should only take about 2-3 minutes.
2. Add the egg yolk and mix until it's just incorporated. Slowly add the ice water, 1 tablespoon at a time, until the dough starts to come together. You may not need all the water. Remove the dough from the bowl, form it into a disk, and wrap it in plastic wrap. Chill in the refrigerator for at least 30 minutes.
3. Prepare the Almond Cream (Frangipane): Once the tart dough is chilled, preheat your oven to 350°F (175°C). In the stand mixer bowl, attach the flat beater attachment. Beat the softened butter and sugar on medium speed until light and fluffy, about 3-4 minutes.
4. Add the egg and vanilla extract, mixing on medium speed until fully combined. Gradually add the almond meal, flour, heavy cream, and a pinch of salt, mixing on low speed until smooth and creamy. Set the almond cream aside while you prepare the tart shell.
5. Once the dough has chilled, roll it out on a lightly floured surface to fit a 9-inch tart pan with a removable bottom. Press the dough gently into the pan and trim any excess. Prick the bottom of the tart crust with a fork to prevent bubbling while baking.
6. Bake the crust in the preheated oven for about 10-12 minutes or until slightly golden. Remove from the oven and allow it to cool slightly.
7. Once the tart shell has cooled, spread the almond cream evenly over the crust. Arrange the pear slices on top of the almond cream. Bake the tart for 35-40 minutes, or until the almond cream is set and lightly golden. The pear slices should be tender but not mushy.
8. Dust with powdered sugar before serving (optional).

Nutritional Value (per slice)

Calories: ~290 | Carbohydrates: 35g | Protein: 4g | Fat: 18g | Fiber: 3g | Sugar: 18g | Sodium: 120mg

Coconut Cream Pie

Ingredients

For the Pie Crust: 1 ¼ cups all-purpose flour | ¼ teaspoon salt | ¼ cup unsalted butter, cold and cut into cubes | 2-3 tablespoons ice water

For the Coconut Cream Filling: 2 cups whole milk | 1 cup heavy cream | ¾ cup granulated sugar | 1/3 cup cornstarch | ¼ teaspoon salt | 4 large egg yolks, beaten | 1 cup shredded coconut, sweetened | 1 teaspoon vanilla extract | 2 tablespoons unsalted butter

For the Topping: 1 cup heavy cream | 2 tablespoons powdered sugar | 1 teaspoon vanilla extract

Prep Time: 30 minutes

Cook Time: 15 minutes

Servings: 8

Directions

1. Attach the flat beater to your stand mixer. In the mixing bowl, combine the flour and salt. Add the cold butter cubes. Mix on low speed until the mixture resembles coarse crumbs. Gradually add the ice water, one tablespoon at a time, mixing until the dough just comes together.
2. Turn the dough out onto a floured surface and shape it into a disc. Wrap in plastic wrap and refrigerate for 30 minutes.
3. After chilling, roll the dough into a 12-inch circle and place it into a 9-inch pie pan. Trim the edges and crimp as desired. Prick the bottom of the dough with a fork to prevent bubbling, then bake in a preheated oven at 375°F (190°C) for 15-20 minutes, or until golden brown.

4. Make the Coconut Cream Filling: In the mixing bowl, combine the whole milk, heavy cream, sugar, cornstarch, and salt. Attach the whisk attachment and mix on medium speed until the ingredients are smooth and well-combined.
5. Place the bowl over medium heat and bring the mixture to a simmer, stirring constantly with a spatula. Once it thickens, reduce the heat to low. Gradually whisk in the beaten egg yolks, a little at a time, then continue to cook for another 2-3 minutes until the custard is thick.
6. Remove the mixture from heat and stir in the shredded coconut, vanilla extract, and butter until the mixture is smooth. Allow the coconut filling to cool slightly, then pour it into the cooled pie crust. Spread it evenly with a spatula. Refrigerate for at least 2-3 hours, or until fully set.
7. Make the Whipped Cream Topping: In the chilled bowl of your stand mixer, pour the heavy cream, powdered sugar, and vanilla extract. Attach the whisk attachment. Whip on medium-high speed until stiff peaks form, about 3-5 minutes. Spread the whipped cream over the chilled coconut cream filling, creating a smooth, even layer.
8. Garnish with additional toasted shredded coconut, if desired, for extra texture and flavor.

Nutritional Value (per slice)

Calories: ~380 | Carbohydrates: 35g | Protein: 4g | Fat: 26g | Fiber: 2g | Sugar: 20g | Sodium: 150mg

Tips: When cooking the custard, be sure not to let it boil too aggressively. Stir constantly to prevent curdling and ensure smooth, creamy filling.

French Silk Pie

Ingredients

For the Pie Crust: 1 ¼ cups all-purpose flour | ¼ teaspoon salt | ½ cup unsalted butter, cold and cut into cubes | 2-3 tablespoons ice water

For the French Silk Filling: 4 oz semisweet chocolate (or bittersweet chocolate), melted and cooled | 1 ¼ cups heavy whipping cream, chilled | ½ cup granulated sugar | 4 oz cream cheese, softened | 1 teaspoon vanilla extract | 2 large eggs (pasteurized, as they are used raw)

Prep Time: 30 minutes

Cook Time: 10 minutes (for pie crust)

Chill Time: 3-4 hours (for the pie to set)

Servings: 8 slices

Directions

1. Attach the flat beater attachment to your stand mixer. In the mixer bowl, combine the flour and salt. Add the cold butter cubes to the bowl, then mix on low speed until the mixture resembles coarse crumbs (about 1 minute).
2. Gradually add the ice water, 1 tablespoon at a time, mixing on low until the dough just starts to come together. Turn the dough onto a floured surface and form it into a ball. Wrap the dough in plastic wrap and refrigerate for at least 30 minutes to chill.
3. After chilling, roll out the dough on a lightly floured surface to fit a 9-inch pie pan. Place the dough in the pan, trimming any excess and crimping the edges to form a decorative border. Pierce the bottom of the dough with a fork to prevent air bubbles while baking.
4. Bake the crust in a preheated oven at 375°F (190°C) for about 10-12 minutes or until golden.
5. Prepare the French Silk Filling: Attach the whisk attachment to your stand mixer. In the stand mixer bowl, beat the chilled heavy whipping cream on high speed until stiff peaks form. Transfer to a separate bowl and set aside.
6. In the stand mixer bowl, combine the softened cream cheese and granulated sugar. Beat on medium speed until smooth and fluffy, about 2-3 minutes. Add the melted and cooled chocolate to the cream cheese mixture and mix until fully combined. Add the vanilla extract and mix to incorporate.
7. Add the eggs, one at a time, and beat for 3-4 minutes until the mixture is light and fluffy. It's essential that the eggs are fully incorporated into the filling, which creates the mousse texture. Gently fold the whipped cream into the chocolate mixture with a spatula, being careful not to deflate the whipped cream. Mix until smooth and well combined.
8. Spoon the chocolate mousse filling into the cooled pie crust and smooth the top with a spatula. Refrigerate the pie for at least 3-4 hours, or until the filling is set and firm.

Nutritional Value (per slice)

Calories: ~500 | Carbohydrates: 45g | Protein: 4g | Fat: 35g | Fiber: 3g | Sugar: 28g | Sodium: 150mg

Cheese and Spinach Tart

Ingredients

For the Crust: 1 ½ cups all-purpose flour | ½ teaspoon salt | ½ cup unsalted butter, chilled and cubed | 3-4 tablespoons ice-cold water

For the Filling: 2 cups fresh spinach, chopped | 1 tablespoon olive oil | 1 cup ricotta cheese | ½ cup feta cheese, crumbled | 2 large eggs | ¼ cup heavy cream | 1 clove garlic, minced | 1 teaspoon fresh lemon juice | Salt and pepper, to taste

Prep Time: 20 minutes

Bake Time: 30-35 minutes

Servings: 6-8 slices

Directions

1. Attach the flat beater attachment to your stand mixer. In the mixer bowl, combine the flour and salt. Add the chilled butter and mix on low speed until the mixture resembles coarse crumbs, about 1-2 minutes. You can stop occasionally to scrape down the sides of the bowl.

2. Gradually add ice-cold water, 1 tablespoon at a time, mixing on low until the dough just begins to come together. Once the dough has formed, remove it from the bowl, wrap it in plastic wrap, and chill for 30 minutes in the refrigerator.
3. Prepare the Filling: Heat the olive oil in a skillet over medium heat. Add the garlic and cook until fragrant, about 1 minute. Add the spinach and cook until wilted and any excess moisture evaporates, about 3-4 minutes. Remove from heat and set aside to cool slightly.
4. In the clean stand mixer bowl, combine the ricotta, feta, eggs, heavy cream, lemon juice, and season with salt and pepper. Use the whisk attachment and mix on low speed until smooth and well combined. Add the cooked spinach mixture to the bowl, and mix until just incorporated.
5. Preheat your oven to 375°F (190°C). Roll out the chilled dough on a lightly floured surface to fit a 9-inch tart pan. Press the dough into the pan and trim any excess. Pour the spinach and cheese filling into the prepared crust, spreading it evenly.
6. Bake for 30-35 minutes, or until the crust is golden brown, and the filling is set and lightly browned on top.

Nutritional Value (per slice)

Calories: ~300 | Carbohydrates: 25g | Protein: 9g | Fat: 20g | Fiber: 2g | Sugar: 3g | Sodium: 450mg

ICE CREAM

54. Strawberry Ice Cream

55. Classic Vanilla Ice Cream

56. Rich Chocolate Ice Cream

57. Biscoff Ice cream

58. Coffee Ice Cream

59. Mint Chocolate Chip Ice Cream

60. Salted Caramel Ice Cream

61. Matcha Green Tea Ice Cream

62. Cookies and Cream Ice Cream

63. Peanut Butter Cup Ice Cream

64. Mango Sorbet (Dairy-Free Option)

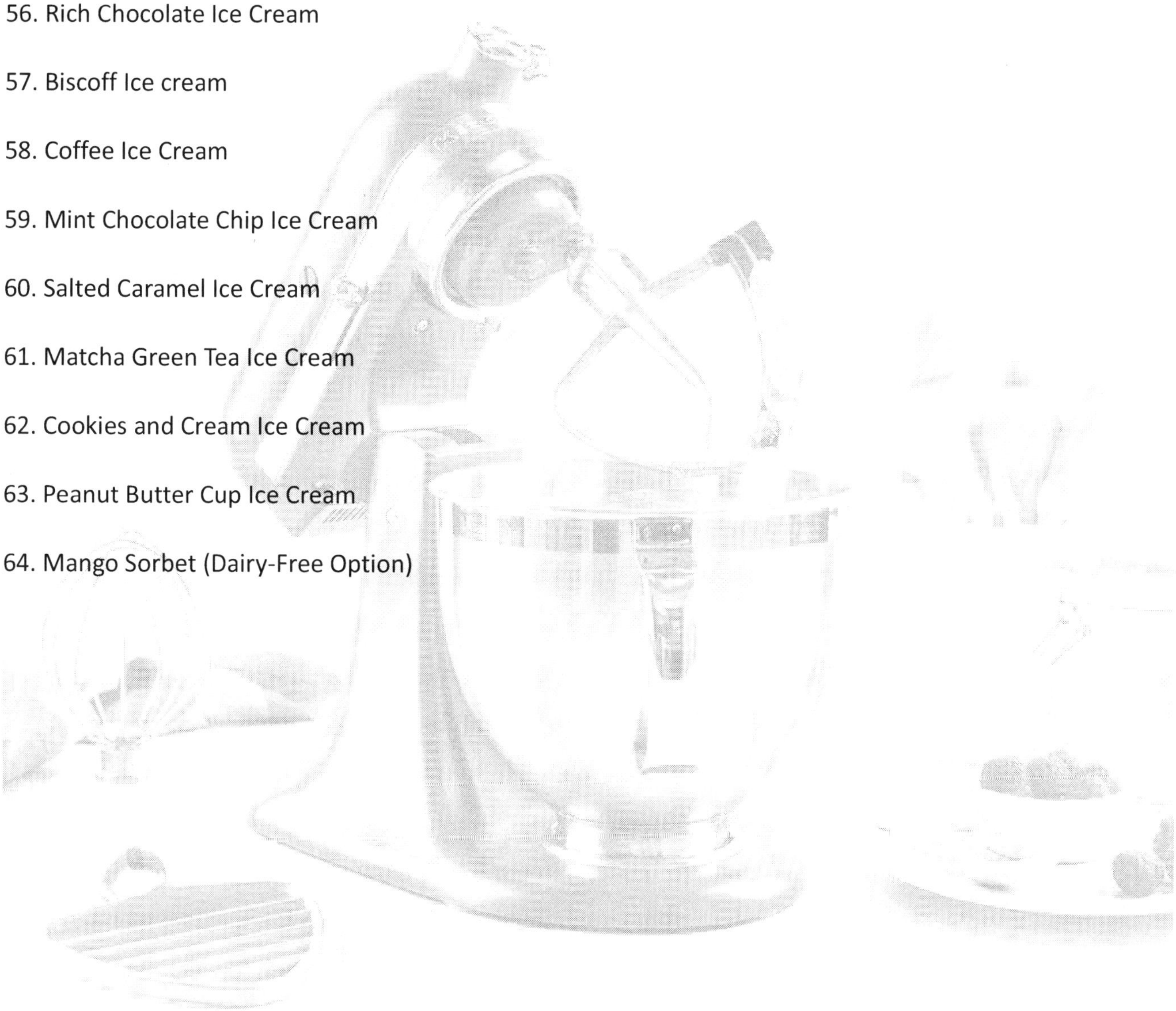

Strawberry Ice Cream

Ingredients

2 cups fresh strawberries, hulled and sliced | 1 cup heavy cream | 1 cup whole milk | ¾ cup granulated sugar | 1 teaspoon vanilla extract | 1 tablespoon lemon juice (optional) | Pinch of salt

Prep Time: 15 minutes

Chill Time: 4-6 hours (for the mixture to chill before churning)

Churn Time: 20-25 minutes

Servings: 6-8

Directions

1. Place the sliced strawberries into a mixing bowl and sprinkle with 2 tablespoons of sugar. Toss them to coat and let them sit for about 10 minutes to release their natural juices.
2. Once the strawberries have softened, use a blender to puree the strawberries until smooth. If you prefer some texture, pulse the strawberries a few times to leave some chunks in the mixture. If desired, you can also add the lemon juice at this stage to enhance the strawberry flavor.
3. Make the Ice Cream Base: In a separate bowl, combine the heavy cream, whole milk, remaining sugar, vanilla extract, and a pinch of salt. Attach the whisk attachment to your stand mixer and mix on medium speed for about 1-2 minutes, until the sugar has dissolved completely and the mixture is smooth.
4. Gently fold the strawberry puree it into the cream mixture. Use a spatula to mix them thoroughly, ensuring the flavors are well combined. At this point, the ice cream base is ready to chill.
5. Transfer the mixture to an airtight container and refrigerate for at least 4 hours, or overnight if possible. Chilling the base ensures the ice cream sets properly when churning.

1. Attach the KitchenAid Ice Cream Maker attachment to your stand mixer (make sure the attachment has been pre-frozen for at least 15 hours).
6. Turn the stand mixer to stir speed (slow speed) and begin pouring the chilled ice cream base into the machine. Let the stand mixer do the work, churning the mixture for about 15-20 minutes, until it reaches a thick, soft-serve consistency.
7. Once the ice cream is churned, transfer it into an airtight container and freeze for an additional 2-4 hours, or until it firms up to your desired consistency.
8. After the ice cream has frozen to the desired consistency, scoop and serve it in bowls or cones. Garnish with extra fresh strawberries, a drizzle of chocolate syrup, or your favorite toppings.

Nutritional Value (per serving)

Calories: ~200 | Carbohydrates: 28g | Protein: 2g | Fat: 10g | Fiber: 1g | Sugar: 24g | Sodium: 30mg

Tips: If you prefer a dairy-free option, substitute the heavy cream and milk with coconut milk or almond milk, keeping in mind that the texture may be slightly different.

Classic Vanilla Ice Cream

Ingredients

2 cups heavy cream | 1 cup whole milk | ¾ cup granulated sugar | 1 tablespoon vanilla extract | 4 large egg yolks | Pinch of salt

Prep Time: 15 minutes

Chill Time: 4 hours (or overnight)

Churn Time: 20-25 minutes

Servings: 6-8

Directions

2. In a medium saucepan, combine the heavy cream, whole milk, and salt. Heat the mixture over medium heat, stirring occasionally, until it is just below simmering point (do not allow it to boil).
3. While the cream mixture is heating, whisk the egg yolks and sugar in a medium bowl until the mixture becomes pale and slightly thickened.
4. Slowly pour a small amount of the hot cream mixture into the egg yolk mixture while whisking constantly. This step, known as "tempering," helps to prevent the eggs from curdling. Gradually add more of the hot cream mixture, whisking continuously.
5. Pour the tempered egg mixture back into the saucepan with the remaining cream mixture. Cook over medium heat, stirring constantly with a wooden spoon or silicone spatula. Keep an eye on the custard until it thickens slightly and coats the back of the spoon, which should take about 5-7 minutes. Be careful not to overheat, as this can cause the custard to scramble.
6. Once the custard has thickened, remove the pan from the heat. Stir in the vanilla extract and then transfer the mixture to a bowl. Let it cool for about 10 minutes before covering and refrigerating it for at least 4 hours, or overnight.
7. Attach the KitchenAid Ice Cream Maker attachment to your stand mixer (make sure the attachment has been pre-frozen for at least 15 hours).
8. Set the stand mixer to low speed and begin slowly adding the chilled custard mixture to the bowl of the Ice Cream Maker. Let the mixer churn the mixture for 20-25 minutes or until it reaches a soft-serve consistency. The colder your mixture, the faster the churning process.
9. Transfer the ice cream to an airtight container. Freeze for at least 2-4 hours to firm up before serving.

Nutritional Value (per serving)

Calories: ~300 | Carbohydrates: 25g | Protein: 4g | Fat: 20g | Fiber: 0g | Sugar: 23g | Sodium: 45mg

Rich Chocolate Ice Cream

Ingredients

2 cups heavy cream | 1 cup whole milk | ¾ cup granulated sugar | 4 large egg yolks | 1 cup good-quality dark chocolate (70% cocoa or higher), finely chopped | 2 tablespoons unsweetened cocoa powder | 1 teaspoon pure vanilla extract

Prep Time: 30 minutes

Chill Time: 4-6 hours (or overnight)

Churn Time: 20-25 minutes

Servings: About 1 quart of ice cream

Directions

1. In a medium saucepan, combine the heavy cream, whole milk, and cocoa powder. Heat over medium heat, stirring occasionally, until the mixture is hot but not boiling. Remove from heat.
2. Place the chopped chocolate in a large mixing bowl. Pour the hot cream mixture over the chocolate and whisk until smooth.
3. Attach the whisk attachment to your stand mixer. In the mixer bowl, whisk the egg yolks and granulated sugar on medium speed until the mixture is thick and pale yellow (about 2-3 minutes).
4. Gradually pour about 1 cup of the warm chocolate mixture into the egg yolk mixture while whisking on low speed. This process tempers the eggs, preventing them from curdling. Slowly pour the tempered egg mixture back into the saucepan with the remaining chocolate mixture.

5. Heat the mixture over medium-low heat, stirring constantly with a wooden spoon or silicone spatula, until it thickens and coats the back of the spoon (about 170°F-175°F or 77°C-80°C). Do not let it boil. Remove from heat and stir in the vanilla extract.
6. Pour the custard through a fine-mesh strainer into a clean bowl to remove any lumps. Cover the custard with plastic wrap, pressing it directly onto the surface to prevent a skin from forming. Refrigerate for at least 4 hours or overnight until thoroughly chilled.
7. Attach the KitchenAid Ice Cream Maker attachment to your stand mixer. Ensure the bowl has been frozen for at least 15 hours before use. Set the mixer to low speed and pour the chilled custard into the frozen bowl. Churn for 20-25 minutes, or until the mixture reaches a soft-serve consistency.
8. Transfer the churned ice cream to an airtight container. Cover the surface with parchment paper or plastic wrap to prevent ice crystals from forming. Freeze for at least 2-4 hours for a firmer texture.

Nutritional Value (per serving)

Calories: ~320 | Carbohydrates: 20g | Protein: 5g | Fat: 26g | Fiber: 3g | Sugar: 18g | Sodium: 30mg

Biscoff Ice cream

Ingredients

2 cups heavy cream | 1 cup whole milk | ¾ cup granulated sugar | 1 teaspoon vanilla extract | ½ cup Biscoff cookie spread (plus extra for drizzling) | 1 cup crushed Biscoff cookies (for folding in)

Prep Time: 15 minutes

Churn Time: 20-25 minutes

Freeze Time: 3-4 hours (or overnight)

Total Time: ~28 hours

Servings: ~1 quart (4 servings)

Directions

1. In a medium saucepan, combine the heavy cream, whole milk, and sugar. Heat over medium heat, stirring constantly, until the sugar has completely dissolved. Do not let the mixture boil. Remove the saucepan from heat and whisk in the vanilla extract and Biscoff cookie spread until smooth. Allow the mixture to cool to room temperature, then cover and refrigerate for at least 4 hours or overnight.
2. Attach the KitchenAid Ice Cream Maker attachment to your stand mixer. Ensure the bowl has been frozen for at least 15 hours before use. Once the ice cream base is thoroughly chilled, pour it into the frozen ice cream maker bowl while the mixer is running on the stir (low) speed. Allow the mixer to churn for 20-25 minutes, or until the mixture thickens to a soft-serve consistency.
3. During the last 2-3 minutes of churning, add the crushed Biscoff cookies. This ensures the cookies are evenly distributed without being overmixed.
4. Transfer the churned ice cream into an airtight container. For an extra touch, drizzle additional melted Biscoff cookie spread over the top and swirl it through with a knife. Freeze for 3-4 hours, or until the ice cream is firm.

Nutritional Value (per serving)

Calories: ~370 | Carbohydrates: 28g | Protein: 4g | Fat: 25g | Fiber: 0.5g | Sugar: 24g | Sodium: 100mg

Coffee Ice Cream

Ingredients

2 cups heavy cream | 1 cup whole milk | ¾ cup granulated sugar | 1 tablespoon instant coffee granules (or ½ cup brewed strong coffee, cooled) | 5 large egg yolks | 1 teaspoon vanilla extract

Prep Time: 20 minutes

Chill Time: 4 hours or overnight

Churn Time: 20-25 minutes

Servings: Approximately 1 quart of ice cream

Directions

1. In a medium saucepan, combine the heavy cream, whole milk, and half the sugar (about ⅜ cup). Heat over medium heat, stirring occasionally, until the sugar dissolves and the mixture is hot but not boiling. Dissolve the instant coffee granules into the hot cream mixture (or add the cooled brewed coffee if using). Stir until well combined.
2. In a mixing bowl, whisk the egg yolks with the remaining sugar until the mixture is pale and thick. Slowly add ½ cup of the hot cream mixture into the yolks while whisking continuously to temper them. Gradually whisk the tempered yolks back into the saucepan with the remaining cream mixture.
3. Cook the mixture over medium-low heat, stirring constantly, until it thickens slightly and coats the back of a spoon (about 170-175°F or 75-80°C). Do not let it boil, as this could scramble the eggs. Remove the custard from the heat and stir in the vanilla extract.
4. Strain the custard through a fine-mesh sieve into a clean bowl to remove any cooked egg bits. Cover the bowl with plastic wrap, pressing the wrap directly onto the surface of the custard to prevent a skin from forming. Chill the custard in the refrigerator for at least 4 hours or overnight.
5. Attach the KitchenAid Ice Cream Maker attachment to your stand mixer, ensure the ice cream maker bowl has been frozen for at least 15 hours before use.
6. Set the mixer to stir speed and slowly pour the chilled custard into the ice cream maker attachment. Churn the ice cream for 20-25 minutes, or until it reaches a soft-serve consistency.
7. Transfer the churned ice cream to an airtight container and freeze for 2-4 hours to allow it to firm up. Garnish with a dusting of cocoa powder, chocolate shavings, or whipped cream, if desired.

Nutritional Value (per serving)

Calories: ~260 | Carbohydrates: 20g | Protein: 4g | Fat: 19g | Fiber: 0g | Sugar: 18g | Sodium: 30mg

Mint Chocolate Chip Ice Cream

Ingredients

2 cups heavy cream | 1 cup whole milk | ¾ cup granulated sugar | 1 teaspoon pure peppermint extract | 1 teaspoon vanilla extract | ½ teaspoon green food coloring (optional, for a classic mint color) | 1 cup semisweet chocolate chips or finely chopped chocolate

Prep Time: 15 minutes.

Chill Time: 4 hours or overnight

Churning Time: 20-25 minutes

Servings: 1 quart (4 servings)

Directions

1. In a medium saucepan, combine the heavy cream, whole milk, and granulated sugar. Heat over medium-low heat, stirring occasionally, until the sugar completely dissolves (do not let it boil). Remove from the heat and stir in the peppermint extract, vanilla extract, and food coloring (if using).Transfer the mixture to a bowl and refrigerate for at least 4 hours, or preferably overnight, to ensure it is well chilled.
2. Attach the KitchenAid ice cream maker bowl to the stand mixer. Ensure the bowl has been frozen for at least 15 hours beforehand.
3. Turn on the stand mixer to stir speed (low setting). Slowly pour the chilled ice cream base into the pre-frozen bowl. Let the mixer churn the mixture for 20-25 minutes, or until the ice cream thickens to a soft-serve consistency.
4. With the mixer still running, gradually add the chocolate chips during the last 2-3 minutes of churning. This ensures even distribution throughout the ice cream.

5. Once churned, transfer the ice cream to an airtight container. Freeze for an additional 2-4 hours.
6. Garnish with extra chocolate chips or a sprig of fresh mint for an elegant touch.

Nutritional Value (per serving)

Calories: ~280 | Carbohydrates: 24g | Protein: 4g | Fat: 20g | Sugar: 22g | Fiber: 1g | Sodium: 40mg

Salted Caramel Ice Cream

Ingredients

For the caramel sauce: 1 cup granulated sugar | 4 tablespoons unsalted butter, cubed | ½ cup heavy cream | 1 teaspoon sea salt (or to taste)

For the ice cream base: 2 cups whole milk | 1 cup heavy cream | ½ cup granulated sugar | 5 large egg yolks | 1 teaspoon vanilla extract

Prep Time: 30 minutes

Churn Time: 20-30 minutes

Chill Time: 4-6 hours (for the base) + 2-4 hours (after churning)

Servings: About 1 quart of ice cream

Directions

1. In a heavy-bottomed saucepan, heat the sugar over medium heat, stirring continuously with a heatproof spatula until it melts and turns a deep amber color.

2. Carefully add the butter, stirring until fully incorporated. Slowly pour in the heavy cream (be cautious as it may splatter) and whisk until smooth. Stir in the sea salt and let the sauce cool to room temperature.
3. In a medium saucepan, heat the milk and heavy cream over medium heat until warm but not boiling. Meanwhile, in the stand mixer bowl, attach the whisk attachment and whisk the egg yolks and sugar on medium speed until the mixture becomes pale and thick (about 2 minutes). Gradually pour the warm milk mixture into the egg yolk mixture while whisking continuously to temper the eggs.
4. Transfer the mixture back to the saucepan and cook over low heat, stirring constantly, until the custard thickens and coats the back of a spoon. Do not let it boil. Remove the custard from heat and stir in the vanilla extract and about ½ cup of the prepared caramel sauce. Let the mixture cool slightly before refrigerating for 4-6 hours or overnight.
5. Attach the KitchenAid Ice Cream Maker attachment to your stand mixer. Ensure the bowl has been frozen for at least 15 hours in advance. Pour the chilled custard base into the frozen ice cream maker bowl and churn on low speed for 20-30 minutes, or until the ice cream reaches a soft-serve consistency. During the last few minutes of churning, drizzle in an additional 2-3 tablespoons of caramel sauce to create a swirl effect.
6. Transfer the churned ice cream to an airtight container. Drizzle more caramel sauce on top if desired and gently swirl it in with a knife. Cover and freeze for at least 2-4 hours until firm.

Nutritional Value (per serving)

Calories: ~320 | Carbohydrates: 28g | Protein: 4g | Fat: 22g | Sugar: 26g | Sodium: 220mg

Tips: Be cautious when working with hot caramel; it can burn quickly. Keep stirring and work on medium heat.

Matcha Green Tea Ice Cream

Ingredients

2 cups heavy cream | 1 cup whole milk | ¾ cup granulated sugar | 2 tablespoons matcha green tea powder | 4 large egg yolks | 1 teaspoon vanilla extract

Prep Time: 30 minutes

Chill Time: 2-4 hours (or overnight)

Churning Time: 20-30 minutes

Servings: About 1 quart of ice cream

Directions

1. In a medium saucepan, combine the whole milk, half of the heavy cream (1 cup), and granulated sugar. Heat over medium heat, stirring occasionally, until the sugar dissolves and the mixture is just about to simmer (do not boil).
2. In a small bowl, whisk the matcha powder with a few tablespoons of the hot milk mixture to create a smooth paste. This prevents clumping when the matcha is added to the base. Add the matcha paste back into the saucepan and stir until fully incorporated.
3. In a separate bowl, whisk the egg yolks. Gradually pour about ½ cup of the hot milk mixture into the yolks while whisking constantly to temper them. Slowly pour the tempered yolks back into the saucepan with the remaining milk mixture, stirring continuously.
4. Cook the mixture over medium-low heat, stirring constantly, until it thickens enough to coat the back of a spoon. Be careful not to let it boil. Remove from heat and stir in the vanilla extract.
5. Pour the custard base through a fine-mesh sieve into a clean bowl to remove any lumps. Stir in the remaining 1 cup of heavy cream. Cover the bowl with plastic wrap, ensuring it touches the surface of the custard to prevent a skin from forming. Refrigerate for at least 2-4 hours, or until completely chilled.
6. Set up the KitchenAid Ice Cream Maker Attachment on your stand mixer. Ensure the bowl has been frozen for at least 15 hours. Turn the stand mixer to Stir (low speed) and slowly pour the chilled custard into the bowl. Let the machine churn for 20-30 minutes, or until the ice cream reaches a soft-serve consistency.
7. Transfer the churned ice cream to an airtight container and freeze for an additional 2-3 hours to firm up. Scoop and serve the ice cream with optional toppings like sweet red bean paste or mochi pieces.

Nutritional Value (per serving)

Calories: ~240 | Carbohydrates: 15g | Protein: 4g | Fat: 18g | Sugar: 14g | Sodium: 40mg

Cookies and Cream Ice Cream

Ingredients

2 cups heavy cream | 1 cup whole milk | ¾ cup granulated sugar | 1 tablespoon vanilla extract | Pinch of salt | 15 chocolate sandwich cookies (such as Oreos), crushed

Prep Time: 10 minutes

Chill Time: 2-3 hours

Churning Time: 20-25 minutes

Freezing Time: 2-4 hours

Servings: 1 quart

Directions

1. In a medium bowl, whisk together the heavy cream, whole milk, sugar, vanilla extract, and a pinch of salt until the sugar is completely dissolved. Cover the mixture with plastic wrap and chill in the refrigerator for at least 2-3 hours or overnight for best results.
2. Attach the ice cream maker attachment to your stand mixer. Ensure the freezer bowl has been frozen for at least 15 hours in advance for proper churning.
3. Remove the ice cream base from the refrigerator and give it a quick stir. Turn the stand mixer to the "stir" setting (low speed) and slowly pour the chilled ice cream mixture into the frozen bowl. Let the mixer churn the ice cream for 20-25 minutes, or until it reaches a soft-serve consistency. During the last 2-3 minutes of churning, add the crushed chocolate sandwich cookies.

4. Transfer the churned ice cream into an airtight container. Smooth the top with a spatula, cover with plastic wrap to prevent ice crystals, and freeze for 2-4 hours, or until the ice cream firms up to your desired consistency.

Nutritional Value (per ½ cup serving)

Calories: ~250 | Carbohydrates: 28g | Protein: 3g | Fat: 14g | Fiber: 1g | Sugar: 22g | Sodium: 110mg

Peanut Butter Cup Ice Cream

Ingredients

2 cups heavy cream | 1 cup whole milk | ¾ cup granulated sugar | ½ cup creamy peanut butter | 1 teaspoon vanilla extract | Pinch of salt | 1 cup chopped peanut butter cups (about 12 small cups)

Prep Time: 20 minutes

Chill Time: 4-6 hours (or overnight)

Churn Time: 20-25 minutes

Freeze Time: 2-3 hours (for firm texture)

Servings: 6-8 servings

Directions

1. Freeze the KitchenAid Ice Cream Maker Attachment for at least 15 hours prior to use. It's essential that the bowl is completely frozen for the best results.
2. Attach the whisk attachment to the stand mixer. In the mixer bowl, combine the granulated sugar, peanut butter, and a pinch of salt. Mix on medium speed until smooth and well-blended. Gradually pour in the heavy cream and whole milk while mixing on low speed until fully combined. Add the vanilla extract and mix for an additional minute.
3. Transfer the ice cream base to a sealed container and refrigerate for at least 4-6 hours, or overnight.
4. Attach the frozen ice cream bowl and the dasher to the stand mixer. Set the mixer to Stir (lowest speed) and slowly pour the chilled ice cream base into the bowl. Churn for about 20-25 minutes, or until the mixture reaches a soft-serve consistency.
5. During the last 2-3 minutes of churning, add the chopped peanut butter cups. Let the mixer fold them evenly into the ice cream.
6. Transfer the churned ice cream to an airtight container. Cover the surface with plastic wrap or parchment paper to prevent ice crystals from forming. Freeze for 2-3 hours to achieve a scoopable texture.

Nutritional Value (per serving)

Calories: ~320 | Carbohydrates: 28g | Protein: 6g | Fat: 22g | Fiber: 1g | Sugar: 23g | Sodium: 120mg

Tips: For a smoother texture, strain the ice cream base before chilling to remove any undissolved sugar or peanut butter lumps.

Ingredients

4 cups ripe mangoes, peeled, pitted, and diced (about 4 large mangoes) | ½ cup granulated sugar (adjust to taste) | ½ cup water | 2 tablespoons lime juice | Pinch of salt

Prep Time: 20 minutes

Chill Time: 2 hours

Churn Time: 20 minutes

Servings: 6-8 servings

Directions

1. Place the diced mangoes, sugar, water, lime juice, and salt in a blender or food processor. Blend until smooth. Taste the puree and adjust the sweetness with more sugar or lime juice, if needed. The mixture should be slightly sweeter than desired, as freezing will dull the sweetness. Strain the puree through a fine-mesh sieve into a bowl to remove any fibrous bits for a smoother texture.
2. Cover the bowl with plastic wrap and refrigerate the mango puree for at least 2 hours, or until thoroughly chilled.
3. Ensure the KitchenAid ice cream maker attachment bowl has been frozen for at least 15 hours prior to use. Attach the frozen bowl to the stand mixer and set up the dasher (paddle) attachment.
4. Turn the stand mixer to the "Stir" speed and slowly pour the chilled mango puree into the ice cream maker attachment. Let the mixer churn the sorbet for about 15-20 minutes, or until it thickens to a soft-serve consistency.
5. Transfer the churned mango sorbet to an airtight container. Place the container in the freezer for at least 2 hours to firm up before serving.
6. Scoop the sorbet into bowls or cones. Garnish with fresh mint leaves, lime zest, or additional diced mango.

Nutritional Value (per serving)

Calories: ~110 | Carbohydrates: 28g | Protein: 1g | Fat: 0g | Fiber: 2g | Sugar: 25g | Sodium: 15mg

COOKIES

65. Double Berry Chocolate Granola Bars

66. Chocolate Tahini Cookies

67. Lemon & Lime Macarons

68. Almond Macarons With Dark Chocolate Ganache Filling

69. S'mores Ice Cream Bars

70. Peanut Butter And Jelly Bars

71. Chocolate Chip Cookies

72. No Bake White Chocolate Peppermint Oreo Truffles

73. Lemon Lavender Cookies

74. Salted Caramel Ginger Cookies

75. Nutella Oatmeal Cookies

76. Classic Butter Biscuits

77. Chocolate Chunk Brownies

Double Berry Chocolate Granola Bars

Ingredients

2 cups rolled oats | ½ cup unsweetened applesauce | ¼ cup honey or maple syrup | ½ cup almond butter (or peanut butter) | ½ cup dark chocolate chips | ½ cup dried cranberries | ½ cup dried blueberries | ¼ cup chia seeds (optional) | ½ teaspoon vanilla extract | Pinch of salt

Prep Time: 10 minutes

Bake Time: 15 minutes

Servings: 12-16 granola bars

Directions

1. Preheat the oven to 350°F (175°C). Line an 8x8-inch square baking pan with parchment paper, leaving some extra paper overhanging for easy removal later.
2. Attach the Flat Beater attachment to your stand mixer. In the mixing bowl, combine the applesauce, honey (or maple syrup), almond butter, vanilla extract, and a pinch of salt. Turn the stand mixer to low speed and mix for about 1-2 minutes until smooth and well combined.
3. Add the rolled oats, chia seeds (if using), dried cranberries, dried blueberries, and chocolate chips to the wet mixture. Turn the mixer to stir speed and mix until all ingredients are evenly distributed.
4. Transfer the granola mixture into the prepared baking pan. Use a spatula or the back of a spoon to firmly press the mixture into the pan, ensuring an even layer. This will help the granola bars hold together after baking.
5. Place the pan in the preheated oven and bake for 12-15 minutes or until the edges are lightly golden and the bars feel firm to the touch. Allow the bars to cool in the pan for 10 minutes before lifting them out using the overhanging parchment paper.

6. Let the bars cool completely on a wire rack before slicing them into squares or rectangles.

Nutritional Value (per serving)

Calories: ~150 | Carbohydrates: 20g | Protein: 4g | Fat: 7g | Fiber: 3g | Sugar: 10g | Sodium: 45mg

Chocolate Tahini Cookies

Ingredients

1 cup (2 sticks) unsalted butter, softened | ½ cup tahini (preferably smooth) | 1 cup brown sugar, packed | 1 large egg | 2 teaspoons vanilla extract | 1 ½ cups all-purpose flour | ½ cup unsweetened cocoa powder | 1 teaspoon baking soda | ½ teaspoon salt | 1 cup semi-sweet chocolate chips

Prep Time: 15 minutes

Chill Time: 30 minutes

Bake Time: 10-12 minutes

Servings: 24 cookies

Directions

1. Attach the flat beater to your sand mixer and place the softened butter and tahini in the mixing bowl. Start mixing on low speed to combine, then increase to medium speed and cream the butter and tahini together until smooth and fluffy, about 2-3 minutes.
2. With the mixer running on medium speed, gradually add the brown sugar, then the egg, and vanilla extract. Mix for an additional 2 minutes, ensuring the mixture is well incorporated.

3. Combine the Dry Ingredients: In a separate bowl, whisk together the flour, cocoa powder, baking soda, and salt. Slowly add the dry ingredients to the wet mixture while mixing on low speed. Mix until the dough begins to come together. Be careful not to overmix, as this can lead to dense cookies.
4. Turn off the stand mixer and fold in the chocolate chips by hand or using the stand mixer on the lowest speed with the flat beater. This ensures the chips are evenly distributed throughout the dough without overworking it.
5. Wrap the dough in plastic wrap and refrigerate for at least 30 minutes. Chilling helps prevent the cookies from spreading too much while baking and results in a chewier texture.
6. Preheat the oven to 350°F (175°C) and line a baking sheet with parchment paper.
7. After chilling, scoop tablespoon-sized portions of dough and roll them into balls. Place them about 2 inches apart on the prepared baking sheet. Flatten each dough ball slightly with your fingers or the back of a spoon.
8. Bake the cookies for 10-12 minutes, or until the edges are set and the centers are still soft. They will continue to firm up as they cool.

Nutritional Value (per serving)

Calories: ~210 | Carbohydrates: 26g | Protein: 3g | Fat: 12g | Fiber: 2g | Sugar: 17g | Sodium: 90mg

Tips:

- ✓ If the dough feels too soft after mixing, chill it for an additional 10 minutes before scooping.
- ✓ Store the cookies in an airtight container at room temperature for up to one week. For longer storage, freeze the cookies in a zip-top bag for up to 3 months.

Lemon & Lime Macarons

Ingredients

For the Macaron Shells: 1 ½ cups powdered sugar | 1 cup almond flour | 3 large egg whites (room temperature) | ¼ cup granulated sugar| ¼ teaspoon cream of tartar | 1 teaspoon lemon zest | 1 teaspoon lime zest | Yellow and green food coloring (optional)

For the Lemon & Lime Buttercream Filling: 1 cup unsalted butter, softened | 2 cups powdered sugar | 2 tablespoons lemon juice | 1 tablespoon lime juice | 1 teaspoon lemon zest | 1 teaspoon lime zest | Pinch of salt

Prep Time: 30 minutes.

Cook Time: 15 minutes

Cooling Time: 1 hour (for shells)

Chill Time: 2-3 hours (for filling)

Servings: 20-25 macarons (depending on size)

Directions

1. Preheat the oven to 300°F (150°C). Line two baking sheets with parchment paper. Sift the powdered sugar and almond flour together into a bowl, ensuring there are no lumps. Set aside.
2. Attach the whisk attachment to the stand mixer. Place the egg whites in the bowl and beat on medium speed until they become foamy. Add the cream of tartar and continue beating until soft peaks form. Gradually add the granulated sugar and continue to beat until stiff peaks form. The meringue should be glossy and firm.
3. Gently fold the almond flour mixture into the meringue using a spatula, being careful not to deflate the batter. Add the lemon and lime zest and gently fold them in as well. If desired, divide the batter into two portions, adding yellow food coloring to one and green food coloring to the other to create a two-tone effect.
4. Transfer the macaron batter into a piping bag fitted with a round tip. Pipe small, even circles (about 1 inch in diameter) onto the prepared baking sheets, leaving space between each one. Tap the baking sheet on the counter to release any air bubbles. Let the macarons sit at room temperature for about 30 minutes, allowing them to form a skin.
5. Bake the macarons in the preheated oven for 12-15 minutes, or until the tops are firm and a "foot" has formed around the base of each macaron.
6. Make the Buttercream Filling: Attach the paddle attachment to your stand mixer. Beat the softened butter on medium speed for 2-3 minutes until it is light and fluffy. Gradually add the powdered sugar, a little at a time, and continue beating until smooth. Add the lemon juice, lime juice, lemon zest, and lime zest, and beat until well combined. Taste and adjust the sweetness or citrus flavor as

desired. If the buttercream is too thick, you can add a little more lemon or lime juice to reach your desired consistency.

7. Pair up the macaron shells by size. Pipe a small amount of the lemon & lime buttercream onto the flat side of one shell. Gently press the second shell on top, twisting slightly to spread the filling evenly. Let the macarons rest in the refrigerator for at least 2-3 hours to allow the flavors to meld together and the filling to set.

Nutritional Value (per serving)

Calories: ~80-100 (per macaron) | Carbohydrates: 15g | Protein: 1g | Fat: 3g | Fiber: 0g | Sugar: 14g | Sodium: 10mg

Almond Macarons With Dark Chocolate Ganache Filling

Ingredients

For the Macaron Shells: 1 ¾ cups powdered sugar | 1 cup almond flour | 3 large egg whites, at room temperature | ¼ cup granulated sugar | 1 teaspoon vanilla extract (optional) | A pinch of salt | Gel food coloring (optional)

For the Dark Chocolate Ganache Filling: 4 oz dark chocolate (at least 60% cocoa) | ½ cup heavy cream | 2 tablespoons unsalted butter, room temperature

Prep Time: 20 minutes

Bake Time: 12-15 minutes

Servings: Approximately 20 macarons (40 shells)

Directions

1. Preheat your oven to 300°F (150°C) and line two baking sheets with parchment paper or silicone mats. In the bowl of your stand mixer, sift together the powdered sugar and almond flour. This ensures a smooth batter without any lumps.
2. Using the whisk attachment, beat the egg whites on medium speed until frothy, about 1 minute. Add a pinch of salt and gradually add the granulated sugar. Continue beating at high speed until stiff peaks form, around 3-5 minutes. The meringue should be glossy and hold its shape when the whisk is lifted.
3. If using, add a few drops of gel food coloring at this point and mix on low speed until the color is evenly distributed. Gently fold in the almond flour and powdered sugar mixture into the meringue using a spatula. The goal is to achieve a smooth batter that flows like lava. Be careful not to deflate the meringue too much.
4. Transfer the macaron batter into a piping bag fitted with a round tip (about ¼-inch wide). Pipe small, uniform circles (about 1 ½ inches in diameter) onto the prepared baking sheets, leaving space between each one.
5. Tap the baking sheets on the counter a few times to remove air bubbles from the batter. Let the macarons sit at room temperature for about 30 minutes to form a dry skin on top. This makes the macarons form their signature "feet" during baking.
6. Bake the macarons in the preheated oven for 12-15 minutes, or until they are set and can be easily lifted from the parchment paper. Rotate the baking sheets halfway through to ensure even baking.
7. Prepare the Filling: While the macaron shells cool, heat the heavy cream in a small saucepan over medium heat until it begins to simmer. Remove the pan from the heat and add the chopped dark chocolate. Stir until the chocolate is fully melted and smooth. Add the butter and stir until the ganache is glossy and smooth. Let it cool to room temperature, then refrigerate for about 20-30 minutes to thicken it to a spreadable consistency.
8. Once the macaron shells have cooled, pair them up according to size. Using a small spoon or a piping bag, spread or pipe a generous amount of ganache onto the flat side of one shell.
9. Gently sandwich the second shell on top, pressing lightly to spread the filling to the edges. Let the assembled macarons rest in the refrigerator for at least 24 hours before serving.

Nutritional Value (per macaron)

Calories: ~90 | Carbohydrates: 10g | Protein: 1g | Fat: 5g | Fiber: 1g | Sugar: 8g | Sodium: 5mg

Tips: If the macarons are browning too quickly, reduce the oven temperature to 275°F (135°C).

S'mores Ice Cream Bars

Ingredients

For the Crust: 1 ½ cups graham cracker crumbs | ¼ cup granulated sugar | ½ cup unsalted butter, melted| Pinch of salt

For the Ice Cream Filling: 2 cups heavy cream | 1 cup whole milk | 1 cup marshmallow fluff | ½ cup granulated sugar | 1 tsp vanilla extract

For the Chocolate Layer: 1 cup semi-sweet chocolate chips | 2 tbsp unsalted butter | ¼ cup heavy cream

Prep Time: 20 minutes

Freeze Time: 4 hours (or overnight)

Servings: 12 bars

Directions

1. In a bowl, combine the graham cracker crumbs, sugar, melted butter, and a pinch of salt. Use the stand mixer with the paddle attachment to mix the crust ingredients until they are evenly incorporated.
2. Press the graham cracker mixture firmly into the bottom of a greased 9x9-inch pan, creating an even layer. Use the back of a spoon to pack it down tightly. Place the pan in the freezer while preparing the ice cream filling.
3. Make the Ice Cream Filling: In the stand mixer bowl, combine the heavy cream, whole milk, marshmallow fluff, sugar, and vanilla extract. Attach the whisk attachment and mix on medium speed until everything is smooth and the mixture is slightly thickened, about 2-3 minutes.
4. Carefully remove the bowl and gently pour the ice cream mixture over the prepared graham cracker crust, spreading it out evenly with a spatula. Place the pan back into the freezer and let the filling freeze for at least 4 hours, or until it is set and firm.

5. Prepare the Chocolate Layer: In a small saucepan, combine the semi-sweet chocolate chips, butter, and heavy cream over medium heat. Stir continuously until the mixture is smooth and the chocolate has completely melted. Allow the chocolate to cool for a few minutes, then pour it over the frozen ice cream layer. Spread it out evenly with a spatula. Return the pan to the freezer for another 30-60 minutes, or until the chocolate layer has hardened.
6. Once the bars are fully frozen and set, remove them from the freezer. Use a sharp knife to cut the bars into squares or rectangles, depending on your preference.

Nutritional Value (per serving)

Calories: ~270 | Carbohydrates: 34g | Protein: 3g | Fat: 16g | Fiber: 1g | Sugar: 22g | Sodium: 90mg

Tips:

- ✓ For an added touch, you can sprinkle some mini marshmallows or more graham cracker crumbs over the chocolate layer before freezing.
- ✓ Run your knife under hot water between cuts to make slicing easier.

Peanut Butter And Jelly Bars

Ingredients

1 cup creamy peanut butter | ½ cup unsalted butter, softened | ¾ cup brown sugar, packed | ¼ cup granulated sugar | 1 teaspoon vanilla extract | 2 large eggs | 1 ½ cups all-purpose flour | 1 teaspoon baking

powder | ¼ teaspoon salt | ½ cup peanut butter chips (optional) | ½ cup jelly or jam (your choice of flavor, such as grape or strawberry)

Prep Time: 10 minutes

Baking Time: 30-35 minutes

Servings: 16 bars

Directions

1. Preheat the oven to 350°F (175°C). Grease and flour an 8x8-inch baking pan, or line it with parchment paper for easier removal of the bars after baking.
2. Attach the flat beater to your stand mixer and place the softened butter and peanut butter in the mixer bowl. Start mixing on low speed to combine, then increase to medium speed for about 2 minutes until the mixture is light and fluffy. This helps incorporate air into the batter for a better texture.
3. Add the brown sugar, granulated sugar, and vanilla extract to the mixer bowl. Mix on medium speed until fully combined, this should take about 1-2 minutes. Add the eggs, one at a time, allowing each egg to fully incorporate before adding the next.
4. Add the Dry Ingredients: In a separate bowl, whisk together the flour, baking powder, and salt. Gradually add the dry ingredients to the mixer bowl, starting on low speed and gradually increasing to medium speed. Mix until just combined—be careful not to overmix. If you're using peanut butter chips, fold them in at this stage.
5. Transfer about two-thirds of the dough into the prepared baking pan, spreading it into an even layer with a spatula. Using a spoon, drop spoonfuls of your jam or jelly over the dough. Then, use a knife or offset spatula to swirl the jelly into the dough, creating a marble effect. Take the remaining dough and gently drop spoonfuls over the jam, spreading it out evenly to cover the entire surface.
6. Place the pan in the preheated oven and bake for 30-35 minutes, or until the top is golden brown and a toothpick inserted into the center comes out clean.
7. Once cooled, cut the bars into squares and serve. These can be stored in an airtight container for up to a week.

Nutritional Value (per serving)

Calories: 220 | Carbohydrates: 27g | Protein: 4g | Fat: 12g | Fiber: 1g | Sugar: 16g | Sodium: 160mg

Chocolate Chip Cookies

Ingredients

2 ¼ cups all-purpose flour | 1 teaspoon baking soda | 1 teaspoon salt | 1 cup unsalted butter, softened | ¾ cup granulated sugar | ¾ cup packed light-brown sugar | 1 teaspoon pure vanilla extract | 2 large eggs | 2 cups semisweet and/or milk chocolate chips (or a mix of both)

Prep Time: 10 minutes

Cook Time: 10-12 minutes per batch

Chill Time: Optional, 30 minutes

Servings: 24-30 cookies

Directions

1. In a small bowl, combine the all-purpose flour, baking soda, and salt. Whisk together to ensure an even distribution of the leavening agent and salt. Set aside.
2. Attach the flat beater to your stand mixer. Place the unsalted butter, granulated sugar, and brown sugar into the mixer bowl. Set the stand mixer to medium speed and mix for 2-3 minutes until the butter is light and fluffy. Add the vanilla extract and eggs one at a time, mixing well after each addition. Continue mixing until fully incorporated.
3. Gradually add the flour mixture to the wet ingredients in the bowl. Set the stand mixer to low speed to prevent flour from flying out of the bowl. Mix until just combined.
4. Turn the stand mixer to stir speed and add the chocolate chips (or combination of chips). Mix for 30 seconds, or until the chocolate chips are evenly distributed throughout the dough.
5. If you prefer thicker, chewier cookies, refrigerate the dough for 30 minutes to an hour. Chilling helps the dough firm up and prevents the cookies from spreading too thin while baking.

6. Preheat your oven to 350°F (175°C). Line a baking sheet with parchment paper or a silicone baking mat for easy cleanup. Use a cookie scoop or tablespoon to drop dough balls onto the prepared baking sheet, spacing them about 2 inches apart. Bake for 10-12 minutes, or until the edges are golden brown and the centers are soft. For chewier cookies, aim for slightly underbaked cookies, as they will continue to firm up as they cool.

Nutritional Value (per cookie)

Calories: 190 | Carbohydrates: 24g | Protein: 2g | Fat: 10g | Fiber: 1g | Sugar: 15g | Sodium: 115mg

Tips: For uniformly sized cookies, use a cookie scoop. This ensures consistent baking and presentation.

No Bake White Chocolate Peppermint Oreo Truffles

Ingredients:

36 chocolate sandwich cookies (e.g., Oreos), finely crushed | 8 oz (225g) cream cheese, softened | ½ teaspoon peppermint extract | 16 oz (450g) white chocolate, melted | Crushed peppermint candies or sprinkles for topping

Preparation Time: 20 minutes

Chilling Time: 1 hour

Servings: Makes about 24 truffles.

Instructions:

1. Secure the mixing bowl to the stand mixer and attach the flat beater. Add the crushed cookies and softened cream cheese to the bowl. Mix on Speed 4 until the ingredients combine into a smooth, sticky dough. Add the peppermint extract and mix briefly to incorporate.
2. Scoop out tablespoon-sized portions of the mixture and roll them into smooth balls using your hands. Place the balls on a parchment-lined baking sheet.
3. Transfer the baking sheet to the refrigerator and chill the truffles for at least 1 hour, or until firm.
4. Melt the white chocolate in a microwave-safe bowl or using a double boiler. Dip each chilled truffle into the melted chocolate, ensuring it is fully coated. Use a fork or dipping tool to remove the truffle, allowing excess chocolate to drip off.
5. Before the chocolate sets, sprinkle crushed peppermint candies or festive sprinkles on top for decoration.
6. Place the coated truffles back on the parchment-lined tray and refrigerate until the chocolate is fully set, about 10–15 minutes.

Nutritional Value (Per Truffle):

Calories: ~150 | Carbohydrates: ~18g | Protein: ~2g | Fat: ~8g

Tips:

- ✓ Use a food processor attachment to crush the cookies evenly if you prefer.
- ✓ For easier handling, chill your hands with ice water before rolling the truffles.
- ✓ Swap white chocolate for dark or milk chocolate if desired.

Lemon Lavender Cookies

Ingredients

1 ¾ cups all-purpose flour | 1 tablespoon dried culinary lavender, crushed | 1 teaspoon baking powder | ½ teaspoon baking soda | ¼ teaspoon salt | 1 cup unsalted butter, softened | 1 cup granulated sugar| 1 large egg | 1 tablespoon fresh lemon zest | 2 tablespoons fresh lemon juice | 1 teaspoon vanilla extract

Prep Time: 15 minutes

Chill Time: 1 hour

Baking Time: 12-15 minutes

Servings: 24 cookies

Directions

1. In a medium bowl, whisk together the all-purpose flour, crushed lavender, baking powder, baking soda, and salt. Set aside.
2. Attach the flat beater to your stand mixer. Place the softened butter and granulated sugar into the mixing bowl. Beat on medium speed for 3-4 minutes, or until the mixture is light and fluffy. The stand mixer's speed and even mixing will ensure a smooth texture without lumps.
3. Add the egg, lemon zest, lemon juice, and vanilla extract to the creamed butter mixture. Mix on medium-low speed until fully combined, scraping down the sides of the bowl as needed to ensure even incorporation.
4. Gradually add the dry ingredients to the wet mixture in small batches. Mix on low speed to avoid flour flying out of the bowl. Continue until the dough just comes together, ensuring no dry flour remains.
5. Divide the dough into two portions and wrap each in plastic wrap. Chill the dough in the refrigerator for at least 1 hour, allowing the flavors to meld and making the dough easier to handle.
6. Preheat the oven to 350°F (175°C) and line a baking sheet with parchment paper. After chilling, scoop tablespoon-sized portions of dough and roll them into balls. Place them about 2 inches apart on the baking sheet. Lightly press down on each dough ball with a fork or your fingers to flatten them slightly.
7. Bake the cookies for 12-15 minutes, or until the edges are lightly golden.

Nutritional Value (per serving)

Calories: ~140 | Carbohydrates: 18g | Protein: 1g | Fat: 7g | Fiber: 0g | Sugar: 10g | Sodium: 80mg

Salted Caramel Ginger Cookies

Ingredients

2 ½ cups all-purpose flour |1 teaspoon baking soda | 1 teaspoon ground ginger | ½ teaspoon ground cinnamon | ¼ teaspoon ground nutmeg | ½ teaspoon salt | ¾ cup unsalted butter, softened | 1 cup brown sugar, packed | ¼ cup molasses | 1 large egg | ½ teaspoon vanilla extract | ½ cup caramel bits or chopped caramel candies | 1 tablespoon sea salt flakes (for garnish)

Prep Time: 15 minutes

Chill Time: 1 hour

Baking Time: 12 minutes per batch

Servings: 24 cookies

Directions

1. In a medium mixing bowl, whisk together the flour, baking soda, ginger, cinnamon, nutmeg, and salt. Set aside.
2. Attach the flat beater to the stand mixer. In the stand mixer bowl, combine the softened butter and brown sugar. Mix on speed 4 for 2-3 minutes, until the mixture is light and fluffy. Add the molasses, egg, and vanilla extract. Mix on speed 2 until fully incorporated.
3. Gradually add the dry ingredients to the wet mixture on stir speed (speed 1). Mix until just combined. Avoid overmixing to maintain a tender cookie texture. Gently fold in the caramel bits using the stand mixer on stir speed or by hand with a spatula.
4. Transfer the dough to an airtight container or wrap it in plastic wrap. Chill in the refrigerator for at least 1 hour to firm up and enhance the flavor.

5. Preheat the oven to 350°F (175°C). Line baking sheets with parchment paper. Roll the chilled dough into 1 ½-inch balls and place them 2 inches apart on the prepared baking sheets. Lightly press each ball to flatten slightly and sprinkle a pinch of sea salt flakes on top.
6. Bake for 10-12 minutes, or until the edges are set and the centers appear slightly underbaked (they will firm up as they cool).

Nutritional Value (per cookie)

Calories: ~140 | Carbohydrates: 20g | Protein: 2g| Fat: 6g | Fiber: 0.5g | Sugar: 13g | Sodium: 90mg

Nutella Oatmeal Cookies

Ingredients

1 cup (2 sticks) unsalted butter, softened | ¾ cup granulated sugar | ¾ cup brown sugar, packed | 2 large eggs | 1 teaspoon vanilla extract | 1 cup Nutella (plus extra for drizzling or filling, optional) | 1 ½ cups all-purpose flour | 1 teaspoon baking soda | ½ teaspoon salt | 2 cups old-fashioned rolled oats

Prep Time: 15 minutes

Chill Time: 30 minutes (optional for firmer dough)

Bake Time: 10-12 minutes per batch

Servings: Approximately 24 cookies

Directions

1. Attach the flat beater to your stand mixer. Preheat your oven to 350°F (175°C) and line baking sheets with parchment paper.

2. Add the softened butter, granulated sugar, and brown sugar to the mixer bowl. Beat on medium speed until the mixture is light and fluffy, about 2-3 minutes. Add the eggs one at a time, beating well after each addition. Add the vanilla extract and Nutella, mixing until smooth and well combined.
3. In a separate bowl, whisk together the flour, baking soda, and salt. Reduce the mixer speed to low, and gradually add the dry ingredients to the wet mixture. Mix until just combined. Stir in the rolled oats using the mixer on low speed or fold them in manually with a spatula if you prefer a chunkier texture.
4. For firmer cookies, cover the dough and refrigerate for at least 30 minutes.
5. Scoop tablespoon-sized portions of dough onto the prepared baking sheets, spacing them about 2 inches apart. Bake in the preheated oven for 10-12 minutes, or until the edges are golden but the centers remain slightly soft.
6. Drizzle additional warmed Nutella over the cooled cookies for an extra touch.

Nutritional Value (per cookie)

Calories: ~150 | Carbohydrates: 20g | Protein: 2g | Fat: 7g | Fiber: 1g | Sugar: 13g | Sodium: 60mg

Tips: For a stuffed cookie variation, freeze small dollops of Nutella, then encase them in cookie dough before baking.

Classic Butter Biscuits

Ingredients

1 cup (2 sticks) unsalted butter, softened | ¾ cup granulated sugar | 1 large egg | 2 teaspoons vanilla extract | 2½ cups all-purpose flour | ½ teaspoon salt

Prep Time: 15 minutes

Chill Time: 1 hour

Bake Time: 12-15 minutes per batch

Servings: About 24 biscuits (depending on size)

Directions

1. Attach the paddle attachment to your stand mixer. Place the softened butter and granulated sugar in the mixer bowl. Beat on medium speed until the mixture is light and fluffy (about 2-3 minutes). This step incorporates air into the dough, giving the biscuits their tender texture. Reduce the mixer speed to low and add the egg and vanilla extract.
2. In a separate bowl, whisk together the flour and salt. Gradually add the dry ingredients to the wet mixture with the mixer on low speed. Mix just until a dough forms. Avoid overmixing, as this can make the biscuits tough.
3. Divide the dough into two portions, flatten them into discs, and wrap them in plastic wrap. Chill in the refrigerator for at least 1 hour to firm up, making it easier to handle and shape.
4. Preheat your oven to 350°F (175°C). Line baking sheets with parchment paper. Roll out the chilled dough on a lightly floured surface to about ¼-inch thickness. Use cookie cutters or a knife to cut out shapes and transfer them to the prepared baking sheets, spacing them about 1 inch apart.
5. Bake in the preheated oven for 12-15 minutes or until the edges are lightly golden. Serve the biscuits plain, or decorate with icing, sprinkles, or chocolate drizzle once cooled.

Nutritional Value (per biscuit)

Calories: ~120 | Carbohydrates: 14g | Protein: 2g | Fat: 6g | Fiber: 0.5g | Sugar: 6g | Sodium: 40mg

Chocolate Chunk Brownies

Ingredients

1 cup (2 sticks) unsalted butter, melted | 1 cup granulated sugar | 1 cup packed light brown sugar | 4 large eggs | 2 teaspoons vanilla extract | 1 cup all-purpose flour | ¾ cup unsweetened cocoa powder | ½ teaspoon baking powder | ¼ teaspoon salt | 1 ½ cups chocolate chunks (semi-sweet or dark)

Prep Time: 15 minutes

Bake Time: 30-35 minutes

Servings: 12 large brownies or 24 smaller squares

Directions

1. Preheat your oven to 350°F (175°C). Line a 9x13-inch baking pan with parchment paper, leaving an overhang on the sides for easy lifting. Grease lightly.
2. Attach the paddle attachment to the stand mixer. Add the melted butter, granulated sugar, and brown sugar to the mixer bowl. Mix on medium speed for about 2-3 minutes, until the sugars and butter are well combined and creamy. Add the eggs and vanilla extract. Mix on low to medium speed until fully incorporated and the mixture is smooth.
3. In a separate bowl, whisk together the flour, cocoa powder, baking powder, and salt. Reduce the mixer speed to low and gradually add the dry ingredients to the wet mixture, 1/3 at a time, to avoid flour clouds. Mix until just combined; do not overmix.
4. Remove the bowl from the mixer and gently fold in the chocolate chunks using a silicone spatula to evenly distribute them throughout the batter. Transfer the batter into the prepared pan. Use a spatula to spread it evenly, ensuring the surface is smooth.
5. Place the pan in the preheated oven and bake for 30-35 minutes, or until a toothpick inserted into the center comes out with a few moist crumbs (not wet batter). Avoid overbaking for fudgier brownies.

Nutritional Value (per serving)

Calories: ~260 | Carbohydrates: 34g | Protein: 3g | Fat: 12g | Fiber: 2g | Sugar: 25g | Sodium: 60mg

EXTRAS

78. Grated Vegetable Salad
79. Sausage
80. 3-Ingredient Seeded Crackers
81. Panna Cotta (using whipped cream)
82. Chai Doughnuts With Spiced Sugar
83. Cinnamon Roll
84. Chestnut Pavlova
85. Spiced Pavlova with Pumpkin Mousse
86. Pizza
87. Shave Ice Treats
88. Homemade Juice
89. Making Butter from Scratch

Grated Vegetable Salad

Ingredients

2 medium carrots, peeled | 1 medium zucchini | 1 small beet, peeled | 1 cup shredded cabbage (red or green) | ½ cup fresh parsley, chopped | ¼ cup sunflower seeds or pumpkin seeds

Dressing: 3 tablespoons olive oil | 1 tablespoon apple cider vinegar | 1 teaspoon honey or maple syrup | Salt and pepper to taste

Prep Time: 15 minutes

Servings: 4

Directions

1. Connect the KitchenAid slicer/shredder attachment to the stand mixer. Use the medium or fine shredding drum, depending on your desired texture for the vegetables.
2. Turn the stand mixer to speed 4-6, allowing it to work steadily but not too fast. Feed the carrots, zucchini, and beet into the attachment one at a time, gently pressing with the pusher. Collect the grated vegetables in a large mixing bowl.
3. Use the same attachment with the slicing drum (if not pre-shredded) to thinly slice the cabbage for even-sized strips. Add the cabbage to the grated vegetables.
4. Prepare the Dressing: In a small bowl, whisk together olive oil, apple cider vinegar, honey or maple syrup, salt, and pepper. Alternatively, use the whisk attachment on the stand mixer to emulsify the dressing.
5. Pour the dressing over the grated vegetables. Add chopped parsley and sunflower or pumpkin seeds. Toss gently using tongs or a large spoon until the dressing evenly coats the salad.

Nutritional Value (per serving)

Calories: ~120 | Carbohydrates: 9g | Protein: 3g | Fat: 8g | Fiber: 3g | Sodium: 75mg

Tips: Swap vegetables based on availability or preference—such as radishes, bell peppers, or cucumbers.

Sausage

Ingredients

Meat Mixture: 2 pounds pork shoulder (or a mix of pork and beef), cubed | ½ pound pork fat (for juicier sausages), cubed

Seasonings: 2 teaspoons salt | 1 teaspoon black pepper | 1 teaspoon smoked paprika | 1 teaspoon garlic powder | ½ teaspoon ground fennel seeds | ½ teaspoon dried oregano | ¼ teaspoon red pepper flakes (optional, for heat)

Binder: ½ cup ice-cold water

Sausage Casings: Natural hog casings (soaked and rinsed)

Prep Time: 20 minutes

Stuffing Time: 20-30 minutes

Servings: ~12 medium sausages

Directions

1. Chill the meat and fat cubes in the freezer for 30 minutes to ensure they grind easily without smearing. Soak the sausage casings in warm water for at least 30 minutes and rinse thoroughly to

remove excess salt. Attach the Food Grinder attachment to the stand mixer and choose the coarse or fine grinding plate based on your preference.

2. Feed the chilled meat and fat cubes through the grinder attachment while running the mixer on speed 4-6.Collect the ground meat in the mixer bowl.
3. Add the salt, pepper, paprika, garlic powder, fennel seeds, oregano, and red pepper flakes to the ground meat. Switch to the paddle attachment and mix the meat on low speed. Gradually add the ice-cold water until the mixture becomes cohesive and sticky. This ensures proper binding for juicy sausages.
4. Attach the Sausage Stuffer attachment to the mixer and fit the appropriate stuffing tube. Slide the soaked casing onto the tube, leaving a small overhang. Tie a knot at the end of the casing.
5. Turn the mixer to speed 2 and feed the meat mixture into the hopper. Guide the casing as it fills, avoiding overstuffing. Twist the sausage at regular intervals to create individual links.
6. Cook the sausages immediately by grilling, pan-frying, or baking. Alternatively, refrigerate for up to 3 days or freeze for longer storage.

Nutritional Value (per sausage)

Calories: ~220 | Protein: 15g | Fat: 17g | Carbohydrates: 1g | Fiber: 0g | Sodium: 300mg

Tips: For skinless sausages, shape the mixture into patties or rolls without using casings.

3-Ingredient Seeded Crackers

These are a wholesome and easy-to-make snack. Packed with seeds, these crackers are great for dipping, pairing with cheese, or enjoying on their own.

Ingredients

1 cup all-purpose flour (or gluten-free flour for a gluten-free option) | ½ cup mixed seeds (such as sesame, flax, sunflower, or chia) | ⅓ cup water (adjust as needed) | Optional: A pinch of salt for flavor and a drizzle of olive oil for extra crispiness.

Prep Time: 10 minutes

Rest Time: 10 minutes

Bake Time: 15-20 minutes

Servings: About 25-30 crackers

Directions

1. Attach the flat beater to your stand mixer. Add the flour, mixed seeds, and salt (if using) to the bowl of the mixer. Turn the mixer to speed 2 to combine the dry ingredients evenly. Gradually pour in the water while the mixer is running. Continue mixing until the dough comes together and forms a smooth, slightly sticky ball. If the dough is too dry, add water 1 teaspoon at a time.
2. Remove the dough from the mixer bowl, shape it into a disc, and wrap it in plastic wrap. Let the dough rest for 10 minutes at room temperature. This allows the flour to hydrate and makes the dough easier to roll out.
3. Preheat your oven to 375°F (190°C) and line a baking sheet with parchment paper. Place the dough on a lightly floured surface and roll it out thinly, about 1/16 inch thick. Use a knife or a pizza cutter to slice the dough into squares, rectangles, or other shapes. Prick each cracker with a fork to prevent puffing during baking.
4. Transfer the shaped crackers to the prepared baking sheet, leaving a little space between them. Bake for 15-20 minutes, or until the crackers are golden brown and crisp. Rotate the baking sheet halfway through baking for even cooking.

Nutritional Value (per cracker)

Calories: ~35 | Carbohydrates: 5g | Protein: 1g | Fat: 1g | Fiber: 0.5g | Sugar: 0g | Sodium: 10mg (without added salt)

Tips:

- ✓ Customize the seeds to your liking—add pumpkin seeds for a nutty flavor or poppy seeds for a touch of crunch.
- ✓ For an extra crispy texture, brush the crackers lightly with olive oil before baking.

Panna Cotta (using whipped cream)

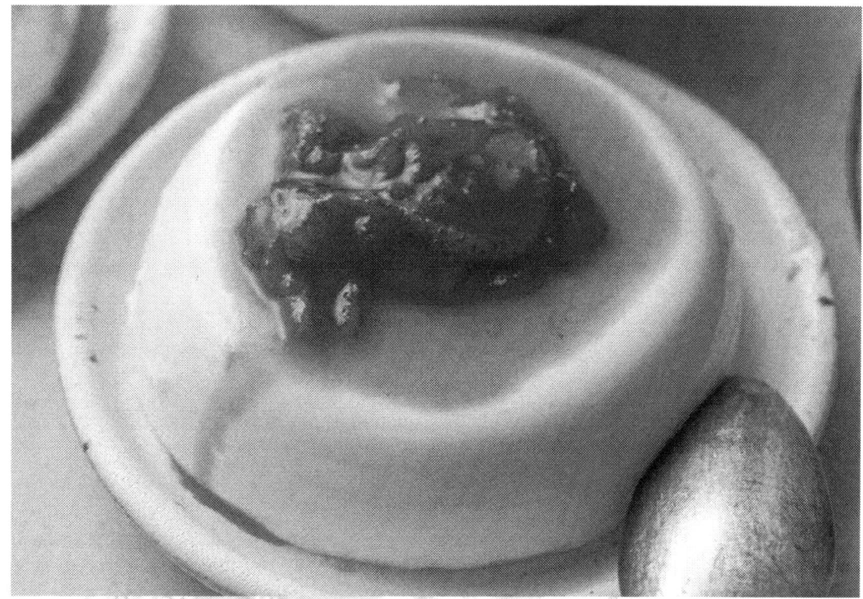

Panna Cotta, an Italian dessert meaning "cooked cream," is a smooth, creamy custard-like treat

Ingredients

2 cups heavy cream | 1 cup whole milk | ½ cup granulated sugar | 2 teaspoons vanilla extract | 2 ½ teaspoons gelatin powder (or 3 sheets of gelatin) | 3 tablespoons cold water | Fresh berries or fruit compote (for topping)

Prep Time: 20 minutes

Chill Time: 4-6 hours (or overnight)

Servings: 6-8

Directions

1. In a small bowl, sprinkle the gelatin powder over the cold water and let it bloom for about 5 minutes. If you're using gelatin sheets, submerge them in cold water for about 5-10 minutes to soften, then remove excess water.
2. In the meantime, pour the heavy cream, whole milk, and granulated sugar into a saucepan. Heat over medium heat, stirring occasionally, until the sugar has completely dissolved and the mixture is just about to simmer. Do not allow it to boil.
3. Once the cream mixture is heated, remove it from the heat and stir in the bloomed gelatin (or softened gelatin sheets) until completely dissolved. Let the mixture cool slightly.
4. Attach the whisk attachment to your stand mixer. Pour the cold heavy cream into the stand mixer bowl. Begin mixing on medium speed, gradually increasing to high speed, and whip the cream until soft peaks form. This typically takes about 2-3 minutes.

5. Once the cream has reached the right consistency, add the vanilla extract and mix for another 20 seconds to incorporate.
6. Once the cream mixture has cooled slightly, fold the whipped cream into the gelatin mixture gently. Use a spatula to combine the two, being careful not to deflate the whipped cream. The result should be a light, fluffy, and smooth custard-like mixture.
7. Pour the panna cotta mixture into individual serving cups, ramekins, or a large mold. Refrigerate for at least 4 hours, or preferably overnight, until it is fully set.
8. Once set, carefully remove the panna cotta from the molds or serve it directly in the cups. Top with fresh berries, a fruit compote, or a drizzle of honey or caramel sauce.

Nutritional Value (per serving)

Calories: ~240 | Carbohydrates: 15g | Protein: 3g | Fat: 20g | Fiber: 0g | Sugar: 14g | Sodium: 60mg

Tips:

- ✓ If the panna cotta is not setting, ensure you're using the correct amount of gelatin. You can also experiment with agar-agar as a plant-based alternative to gelatin.
- ✓ For the perfect whipped cream, make sure your heavy cream is well-chilled before whipping.

Chai Doughnuts With Spiced Sugar

Ingredients

For the Doughnuts: 2 ¾ cups all-purpose flour | 1 teaspoon ground cinnamon | ½ teaspoon ground cardamom | ½ teaspoon ground ginger | ½ teaspoon ground cloves | ½ teaspoon salt | 1 packet (2 ¼ teaspoons) active dry yeast | ¼ cup granulated sugar | ½ cup warm milk (110°F/43°C) | 2 large eggs | 4 tablespoons unsalted butter, softened | 1 teaspoon vanilla extract

For the Spiced Sugar Coating: 1 cup granulated sugar | 1 teaspoon ground cinnamon | ½ teaspoon ground cardamom | ¼ teaspoon ground nutmeg

Prep Time: 20 minutes (plus 1 hour rising time)

Cook Time: 15 minutes

Servings: ~12 doughnuts

Directions

1. Attach the dough hook to your stand mixer. In the mixer bowl, combine warm milk, sugar, and yeast. Let it sit for 5 minutes until the mixture becomes frothy, indicating that the yeast is active.
2. Add the eggs, softened butter, vanilla extract, and spices (cinnamon, cardamom, ginger, cloves) to the yeast mixture. Mix on low speed until just combined.
3. Gradually add the flour and salt, one cup at a time, mixing on medium speed until a soft dough forms. Continue kneading with the dough hook for 5-7 minutes, or until the dough is smooth and elastic. If the dough is too sticky, add a tablespoon of flour at a time. If it's too dry, add a teaspoon of milk.
4. Remove the dough from the mixer, shape it into a ball, and place it in a greased bowl. Cover with a clean kitchen towel and let it rise in a warm, draft-free area for 1 hour, or until doubled in size.
5. Once the dough has risen, transfer it to a lightly floured surface. Roll it out to about ½-inch thickness. Use a doughnut cutter (or a round cookie cutter and a smaller cutter for the center) to cut out the doughnuts. Re-roll scraps to make additional doughnuts. Place the doughnuts on a parchment-lined baking sheet, cover with a kitchen towel, and let them rest for 20 minutes to rise slightly.
6. Heat oil in a deep fryer or heavy-bottomed pot to 350°F (175°C). Carefully lower a few doughnuts into the hot oil, frying for 1-2 minutes per side, or until golden brown. Remove with a slotted spoon and drain on a wire rack or paper towels.
7. Prepare the Coating: In a shallow dish, mix granulated sugar with cinnamon, cardamom, and nutmeg. While the doughnuts are still warm, toss them in the spiced sugar mixture until well-coated.
8. Enjoy the doughnuts fresh and warm with a cup of tea or coffee.

Nutritional Value (per doughnut)

Calories: ~210 | Carbohydrates: 34g | Protein: 4g | Fat: 6g | Sugar: 18g | Sodium: 120mg

Cinnamon Roll

Ingredients:

For the Dough: 3 ¼ cups all-purpose flour | ½ cup sugar | 2 ¼ tsp active dry yeast (1 packet) | ½ tsp salt | ½ cup milk (warm) | ¼ cup unsalted butter, melted | 1 large egg | ½ cup water (lukewarm)

For the Cinnamon Filling: ½ cup brown sugar, packed | 1 tbsp ground cinnamon | ¼ cup unsalted butter, softened

For the Glaze: 1 cup powdered sugar | 2 tbsp milk | ½ tsp vanilla extract

Total Time: 45 minutes

Servings: Makes 1 loaf (8-10 servings)

Directions:

1. In the bowl of the stand mixer, combine the warm water, sugar, and active dry yeast. Let it sit for about 5 minutes, or until it becomes frothy.
2. Add the flour, salt, and melted butter to the bowl with the activated yeast mixture. Attach the flat beater to your stand mixer. On low speed (Speed 2), begin mixing until the dough starts to come together.
3. Add the egg and warm milk, and continue mixing until a dough forms. Once the dough comes together, increase the speed to medium (Speed 4) and knead for about 5-7 minutes, until the dough is smooth and elastic. If the dough is too sticky, add a little more flour (1 tablespoon at a time) until it becomes manageable.
4. Once kneaded, remove the flat beater and switch to the dough hook attachment. Allow the dough to continue kneading on low speed for another 3-4 minutes.

5. Lightly grease a bowl with oil, place the dough in the bowl, and cover it with a damp towel. Let it rise in a warm place for 1-1.5 hours or until it has doubled in size.
6. Prepare the Cinnamon Filling: In a small bowl, combine the brown sugar and cinnamon. Softened butter is then spread over the dough once it's ready for rolling, so be sure to have it at room temperature.
7. Preheat your oven to 350°F (175°C).Once the dough has risen, punch it down to release the air. On a lightly floured surface, roll the dough into a large rectangle (about 12x18 inches).
8. Spread the softened butter evenly over the dough. Then sprinkle the cinnamon-sugar mixture evenly over the buttered dough. Starting at the long end, carefully roll the dough into a tight log. Pinch the seams to seal the roll. Slice the dough into 8-10 even pieces.
9. Place the cinnamon rolls into a greased loaf pan, making sure they are touching each other. Cover the pan with a clean towel and let it rise for 30 minutes.
10. Once the dough has risen, place the loaf pan in the preheated oven. Bake for 25-30 minutes or until golden brown on top.
11. Prepare the Glaze: While it bakes, whisk together the powdered sugar, milk, and vanilla extract in a small bowl until smooth. Adjust the consistency by adding more milk or powdered sugar if needed.
12. Once it is baked, remove it from the oven and allow it to cool slightly before glazing. Drizzle the glaze generously over the warm bread to add a sweet finish.

Nutritional Information (per serving) (approximate):

Calories: 290 | Carbohydrates: 45g | Protein: 4g | Fat: 10g | Fiber: 1g

Chestnut Pavlova

Ingredients

For the Meringue Base: 4 large egg whites (room temperature) | 1 cup granulated sugar | 1 teaspoon cornstarch | 1 teaspoon white vinegar | 1 teaspoon vanilla extract

For the Chestnut Cream: 1 cup chestnut puree (unsweetened) | ½ cup heavy cream | 3 tablespoons powdered sugar | 1 teaspoon vanilla extract

For the Topping: 1 cup heavy cream (for whipping) | 2 tablespoons powdered sugar | Shaved chocolate or chopped candied chestnuts (optional garnish)

Prep Time: 20 minutes

Cook Time: 90 minutes

Cool Time: 2 hours

Servings: 6-8 servings

Directions

1. Preheat your oven to 250°F (120°C). Line a baking sheet with parchment paper and draw a 9-inch circle as a guide for your meringue.
2. In the bowl of your stand mixer, add the egg whites. Attach the whisk attachment and start whipping on medium speed until soft peaks form. Gradually add the sugar, one tablespoon at a time, while continuing to whisk. Increase to high speed and whip until stiff peaks form and the mixture is glossy (about 5-7 minutes). Test by rubbing a small amount between your fingers; it should feel smooth with no sugar granules.
3. Sift the cornstarch over the meringue and gently fold it in with the vinegar and vanilla extract using a silicone spatula.
4. Spoon the meringue onto the parchment paper, spreading it out evenly to fill the circle. Create a slight dip in the center to hold the chestnut cream and toppings later. Place the meringue in the oven and bake for 90 minutes. After baking, turn off the oven and leave the meringue inside to cool completely (at least 2 hours). This helps prevent cracking.
5. Prepare the Chestnut Cream: In a clean stand mixer bowl, combine the chestnut puree, heavy cream, powdered sugar, and vanilla extract. Attach the whisk attachment and whip on medium speed until the mixture is light and fluffy. This should take about 3-4 minutes. Set aside.
6. Whip the Topping: In the same mixer bowl (cleaned and dried), pour in the heavy cream and powdered sugar. Whip on medium-high speed until soft peaks form.
7. Carefully transfer the cooled meringue base to a serving platter. Spoon the chestnut cream into the center of the meringue, spreading it gently. Top with dollops of whipped cream and garnish with shaved chocolate or candied chestnuts, if desired.

Nutritional Value (per serving)

Calories: ~280 | Carbohydrates: 35g | Protein: 4g | Fat: 12g | Fiber: 1g | Sugar: 32g | Sodium: 60mg

Tips:

- ✓ Room temperature egg whites whip more effectively than cold ones, so allow them to sit out for about 30 minutes before starting.
- ✓ To ensure stable peaks, make sure the stand mixer bowl and whisk attachment are clean and free of grease.

Spiced Pavlova with Pumpkin Mousse

Ingredients

For the Spiced Pavlovag: 4 large egg whites, at room temperature | 1 cup granulated sugar | 1 teaspoon ground cinnamon | ½ teaspoon ground nutmeg | ½ teaspoon ground ginger| 1 teaspoon vanilla extract | 1 teaspoon white vinegar | 1 teaspoon cornstarch

For the Pumpkin Mousse: 1 cup heavy whipping cream, chilled | ½ cup canned pumpkin puree | ⅓ cup powdered sugar | ½ teaspoon ground cinnamon | ¼ teaspoon ground nutmeg | ¼ teaspoon ground ginger | 1 teaspoon vanilla extract

Prep Time: 30 minutes

Cook Time: 1 hour

Cooling Time: 1 hour

Servings: 6-8

Directions

1. Preheat your oven to 250°F (120°C). Line a baking sheet with parchment paper and draw a 9-inch circle as a guide.
2. Attach the whisk attachment to your stand mixer. Place the egg whites in the bowl and whisk on medium speed until they form soft peaks (about 3-4 minutes).
3. Increase the speed to high and add the granulated sugar, one tablespoon at a time, ensuring it dissolves completely before adding the next. The mixture should become glossy and form stiff peaks. Gently fold in the cinnamon, nutmeg, ginger, vanilla extract, vinegar, and cornstarch using a spatula. Be careful not to deflate the meringue.
4. Spoon the meringue onto the parchment paper, spreading it into the 9-inch circle. Create a slight well in the center for the mousse topping later.
5. Bake in the preheated oven for 1 hour. Turn off the oven and let the Pavlova cool completely inside to prevent cracking.
6. Make the Pumpkin Mousse: Clean the stand mixer bowl and attach the whisk attachment again. Pour the chilled heavy whipping cream into the bowl and whisk on high speed until soft peaks form. Set aside.
7. Prepare the Pumpkin Mixture: In a separate bowl, mix the pumpkin puree, powdered sugar, cinnamon, nutmeg, ginger, and vanilla extract until smooth.
8. Gently fold the whipped cream into the pumpkin mixture in three additions, ensuring the mousse is light and airy. Chill in the refrigerator for at least 30 minutes.
9. Carefully place the cooled Pavlova onto a serving plate or cake stand. Spoon the chilled pumpkin mousse into the well of the Pavlova, spreading it gently with a spatula.
10. Optional – sprinkle with a dusting of cinnamon, crushed pecans, or a drizzle of caramel sauce for extra flair.

Nutritional Value (Per Serving)

Calories: ~250 | Carbohydrates: 36g | Protein: 4g | Fat: 12g | Fiber: 1g | Sugar: 30g | Sodium: 45mg

Pizza

Ingredients:

3 ¾ cups (450g) all-purpose flour | 1 ½ teaspoons salt | 1 tablespoon sugar | 1 packet (2 ¼ teaspoons) active dry yeast | 1 ⅓ cups warm water (110°F/45°C) | 2 tablespoons olive oil

Preparation Time: 15 minutes

Total Time: ~2 hours 30 minutes

Servings: Makes 2 medium pizzas or 8 slices.

Instructions:

1. In a small bowl, dissolve the sugar in the warm water. Sprinkle the yeast over the water and let it sit for about 5–10 minutes until it becomes foamy. This step confirms that the yeast is active.
2. Attach the mixing bowl to the stand mixer and add the flour and salt. Use the dough hook attachment for this recipe.
3. Turn the stand mixer on low speed (Speed 2). Gradually pour the yeast mixture and olive oil into the flour mixture. Allow the mixer to combine the ingredients until a shaggy dough forms.
4. Increase the speed to medium (Speed 4) and let the dough hook knead the mixture for about 6–8 minutes. To test if the dough is ready, press it gently with your finger. It should spring back slightly. If it's too sticky, add a tablespoon of flour at a time while kneading; if it's too dry, add a teaspoon of water.
5. Remove the dough from the bowl, shape it into a ball, and place it in a lightly greased bowl. Cover it with a damp cloth or plastic wrap and let it rise in a warm place for 1–2 hours or until it doubles in size.

6. Once risen, punch down the dough to release air. Divide it into portions if making multiple pizzas. Roll or stretch the dough into your desired pizza shape and thickness. Add your favorite toppings.
7. Preheat your oven to 475°F (245°C). Place the pizza on a preheated pizza stone or baking sheet and bake for 10–15 minutes or until the crust is golden brown and the cheese is bubbly.

Nutritional Value (Per Slice, Without Toppings):

Calories: ~150 | Carbohydrates: ~30g | Protein: ~5g | Fat: ~2g

Shave Ice Treats

Shave ice, a delightful frozen dessert with origins in Japanese and Hawaiian traditions, is celebrated worldwide in various forms. Unlike the crunchier texture of snow cones, shave ice is known for its light and fluffy consistency, achieved by finely shaving blocks of ice. This treat is typically served with a variety of syrups and flavorings, making it a versatile and refreshing option for any occasion

Ingredients:

Ice molds liquid options: Fresh water, juice (e.g., orange, pineapple), milk, coffee, or any flavored liquid

Basic Fruit Syrup: 1 cup fresh chopped fruit (e.g., strawberries, mango, or pineapple) | 1 cup water | ½ cup sugar | 1 tbsp lemon or lime juice | A pinch of salt

Optional toppings: Fresh fruit (e.g., dragon fruit, mango, pomegranate seeds), toasted coconut, red bean paste, nuts, mochi, or ice cream

Preparation Time: 5 minutes

Freezing Time: 8–12 hours (for ice blocks)

Shaving Time: 5 minutes

Servings: Makes 4 shave ice treats.

Instructions:

1. Fill ice molds to the marked line with your chosen liquid (water, juice, milk, or coffee). Freeze the molds for at least 12 hours, or up to 24 hours for thicker liquids. You can freeze extra molds to have them ready for your next craving.
2. In a saucepan, combine chopped fruit, water, sugar, citrus juice, and a pinch of salt. Bring the mixture to a boil, then reduce to medium-low and simmer for 15 minutes. Blend the mixture until smooth, strain to remove solids, and allow it to cool completely. Store in the refrigerator until needed.
3. Remove frozen ice molds from the freezer and let them sit for 10–15 minutes. The surface should appear glossy, making them easier to shave.
4. Attach the Shave Ice Attachment to your stand mixer's power hub. Load a tempered ice mold into the attachment. Set the mixer to high speed, allowing the fluffy shaved ice to fall into the mixing bowl below.
5. Pour the prepared syrup evenly over the shaved ice. Use as much or as little as desired for sweetness. Add fresh fruit or a sprig of mint for a garnish.

Nutritional Value (Per Serving, Based on Water and Syrup):

Calories: ~80 | Carbohydrates: ~20g | Protein: ~0g | Fat: ~0g

Tips:

- ✓ Use fruit purees for flavored ice blocks to create vibrant, naturally sweetened treats.
- ✓ For layered effects, shave multiple flavored blocks and stack them in a cup.

Homemade Juice

With the Juicer and Sauce Attachment, creating fresh, flavorful juices at home with the stand mixer is both easy and efficient.

Ingredients:

Fruits and vegetables of your choice (e.g., oranges, apples, carrots, celery, ginger, etc.) | Optional: Sweeteners (like honey or agave syrup) or spices (like cinnamon or nutmeg)

Preparation Time: 10 minutes

Juicing Time: 5–10 minutes

Servings: Makes approximately 4 cups (varies based on the produce used).

Instructions:

1. Wash all fruits and vegetables thoroughly. Peel, core, or deseed if necessary (e.g., oranges or apples). Chop larger produce into pieces small enough to fit into the juicer's feed tube.
2. Securely insert the Juicer and Sauce Attachment into the power hub of the stand mixer. Lock it in place to ensure safe and efficient use.
3. Choose the desired pulp strainer (low, medium, or high pulp). Assemble the attachment according to the instructions. Place a large bowl or pitcher beneath the spout to collect the juice.
4. Turn the stand mixer to Speed 6. Feed the fruits and vegetables into the juicer slowly, using the pusher tool to guide them through. The mixer will extract the juice while separating the pulp into a separate container.
5. Taste your fresh juice and adjust to your preference. Add sweeteners or spices if needed. For a smoother juice, strain it further using a fine mesh sieve or cheesecloth.
6. Pour the juice into glasses and serve immediately for maximum freshness and nutritional value.

Nutritional Value (Per Cup, Orange-Carrot-Ginger Blend):

Calories: ~120 | Carbohydrates: ~28g | Fiber: ~2g | Vitamin C: ~100% DV

Tips:

- ✓ Combine different fruits and vegetables for unique flavor profiles (e.g., orange-carrot-ginger or apple-celery-spinach).
- ✓ For a refreshing drink, refrigerate your produce before juicing.
- ✓ Use leftover pulp in smoothies, baking, or composting.

Making butter from scratch is simple and rewarding with the stand mixer. In just a few steps, you'll have fresh, creamy butter and buttermilk to use in your favorite recipes.

Ingredients:

2 cups heavy cream (preferably cold) | ¼ teaspoon salt (optional, for salted butter)

Preparation Time: 5 minutes

Processing Time: 7–10 minutes

Servings: Makes approximately 1 cup of butter and 1 cup of buttermilk.

Instructions:

1. Attach the whisk to the stand mixer and secure the mixing bowl. Pour the heavy cream into the bowl.
2. Set the mixer to Speed 6 and begin whipping the cream. In about 3–5 minutes, the cream will thicken into whipped cream, then break apart as the butterfat separates from the liquid (buttermilk). This is the stage when the mixture will look lumpy.
3. Once the butterfat clumps together and separates from the liquid, stop the mixer. Strain the mixture through a fine-mesh sieve or cheesecloth to collect the buttermilk. Save the buttermilk for baking or cooking.
4. Place the butter back in the bowl. Add cold water to the bowl and mix on Speed 1 to rinse away remaining buttermilk. Drain and repeat until the water runs clear (usually 2–3 rinses).
5. If desired, add salt to the butter and mix on Speed 1 until evenly incorporated.
6. If desired, switch to the flat beater accessory and add your chosen flavorings—such as herbs, garlic, or honey. Mix until combined.
7. Scoop the butter onto wax paper or into a container, shape it, and refrigerate. Fresh butter will keep for up to 1 week in the refrigerator or can be frozen for longer storage.

Nutritional Value (Per Tablespoon):

Calories: ~102 | Carbohydrates: 0g | Protein: 0g | Fat: ~12g

Measurement Conversion Chart

Dry Measurements Chart

Measurement	Equivalent
1 cup	240 ml
1 tablespoon	15 ml
1 teaspoon	5 ml
1 ounce	28.35 grams
1 pound	453.59 grams

Volume

Milliliters (ml)	Teaspoons
5 mL	1 teaspoon
15 mL	3 teaspoons
30 mL	6 teaspoons
60 mL	12 teaspoons
120 mL	24 teaspoons

Oven Temperatures

Measurement	Equivalent
1 cup	240 ml
1 tablespoon	15 ml
1 teaspoon	5 ml
1 ounce	28.35 grams
1 pound	453.59 grams

Baking in Grams

Measurement	Equivalent
1 cup	120 grams
1 tablespoon	15 grams
1 teaspoon	5 grams
1 ounce	28.35 grams
1 pound	453.59 grams

Liquid Conversion

Measurement	Equivalent
1 cup	240 ml
1 fluid ounce	29.57 ml
1 pint	473.18 ml
1 quart	946.35 ml
1 gallon	3,785.41 ml

Weight

Pounds	Kilograms (kg)
1 pound	0.4536 kg
2 pounds	0.9072 kg
5 pounds	2.268 kg
10 pounds	4.536 kg
20 pounds	9.072 kg

A short message from the author

Hey there! How's the book treating you? I'm super curious to know what you think about it! Your thoughts can really make a difference.

Could you spare just a minute to jot down a quick review on Amazon? Even a few sentences would mean the world!

Simply click the link or scan the QR code below and scroll down to get to the *'Write a customer review'* button to leave your review on Amazon

rebrand.ly/stand/mixer/lm

QR code

Thank you for taking the time to share your thoughts!

Made in the USA
Middletown, DE
26 December 2024

68234216R00086